WELSH HISTORY AND ITS SOURCES

People and Protest:
Wales 1815–1880

Contents

Illustrations

Welsh History and its Sources

Welsh History and its Sources is a project conducted at the Open University in Wales from 1985 to 1988 and funded by a Welsh Office Research Development grant. The project gratefully acknowledges the financial support made available by the Secretary of State for Wales.

Project Director: Dr Trevor Herbert

Senior Visiting Fellow: Dr Gareth Elwyn Jones

Steering Committee: Mr O.E. Jones, H.M.I. (Chairman)
                           Professor R.R. Davies, History Department,
                               University College of Wales, Aberystwyth
                           Mr N. Evans, Coleg Harlech
                           Mr D. Maddox, Adviser, Mid Glamorgan LEA
                           Mr A. Evans, Head of History Department,
                               Y Pant Comprehensive School, Pontyclun

Secretary to the Project at the
Open University in Wales: Mrs Julia Williams

Maps and Diagrams

The Contributors

DAVID EGAN is Head of the History Department in Mountain Ash Comprehensive School and tutor-counsellor for the arts foundation course at the Open University in Wales's Pontypridd study centre. He has written numerous articles on recent Welsh History.

NEIL EVANS is a Lecturer in History at Coleg Harlech. He is secretary of Llafur (the Society for Welsh Labour History) and author of a number of articles on modern Welsh history.

TREVOR HERBERT is Sub-Dean, Senior Lecturer in Music and Arts Staff Tutor at the Open University in Wales. He is the author of various Open University course materials and specializes in British music history.

DAVID HOWELL is Senior Lecturer in History at the University College of Swansea. He is an authority on the agrarian history of Wales in the eighteenth and nineteenth centuries. His most recent book is *Patriarchs and Parasites. The Gentry of South West Wales in the Eighteenth Century*, published in 1986.

DAVID J.V. JONES is Reader in History at the University College of Swansea. He is the author of a number of standard works on the history of popular protest and crime in eighteenth and nineteenth-century Britain. His latest book, *The Last Rising. The Newport Insurrection of 1839*, was published in 1985.

GARETH ELWYN JONES is Reader in History Education in the Department of Education, University College of Swansea. He has taught various courses for the Open University in Wales and is currently an arts foundation course tutor-counsellor and assistant staff tutor.

IEUAN GWYNEDD JONES is Emeritus Professor of History at the University College of Wales, Aberystwyth. He has specialized in a pioneering approach to the history of politics and nonconformity in nineteenth-century Wales and has edited in two volumes the Ecclesiastical Census of 1851 as it relates to north and south Wales. His latest book, *Communities*, was published in 1987.

MERFYN JONES is Senior Lecturer in the School of Extension Studies at the University of Liverpool. He is an authority on nineteenth-century social and labour history and in 1981 published *The North Wales Quarrymen, 1874–1922*.

CHRISTOPHER TURNER is Admissions Officer at the University College of Wales, Aberystwyth. In 1979 he completed a doctoral thesis of the University of Wales on 'Revivals and Popular Religion in Victorian and Edwardian Wales'. He has since published papers on the subject in academic journals such as *Llafur*.

The **Debating the Evidence** sections in this book have been written by David Egan.

Preface

This series gives an insight into Welsh history by examining its sources and the ways in which some leading historians use those sources. It is not formally a history of Wales. This volume, for instance, is not a chronological history of Wales in the period 1815–1880, neither is it a comprehensive history in the sense that its themes embrace all of the major issues and events that were important in that period. Readers of this book will, we hope, learn a great deal about Wales in the nineteenth century but they will learn as much about the way in which professional historians interpret the raw materials of history.

The choice of topics for the essays and the collections of documents was determined as much by the nature of the sources relevant to those topics as by the subject matter of the events or issues upon which they are based. Nevertheless, the various sections give a coherent, if not comprehensive, profile of the period. While each essay/sources section is self-contained, the order in which the essays appear is not random. The sections are not in chronological sequence. If they were, an essay which deals with the politics of the mid-century would appear after sections on Rebecca and Chartism. The overall theme is that of the people of Wales following different paths of protest. A commitment to Liberalism and Nonconformity has often been held to be the hallmark of the Welsh nation in the nineteenth century. This image has fostered the notion of 'respectable' protest. In contradistinction, Rebecca in west Wales, the Scotch Cattle and the Chartists in south-east Wales and the tenant farmers and quarrymen of north Wales pursued less constitutional forms of protest. Our sequencing, therefore, attempts to polarize the twin approaches but, in so doing, poses the question as to whether this distinction was a real one, and how far each represented the 'true' Wales of the nineteenth century.

Fundamental changes in living conditions in nineteenth-century Wales resulted from urbanization. This is dealt with by Neil Evans in the first section in terms of the effects of urbanization on the old and emerging societies in Wales.

Within a matter of decades, Wales was transformed from a country in which the majority of inhabitants lived in rural areas to one whose population lived predominantly in urban areas. Problems of disease and poverty were not confined to towns but the density of population in towns made the problems particularly significant and acute.

In Essay/Sources B, Professor Ieuan Gwynedd Jones examines the politics through which, by the second half of the century, Wales was assuming a clear identity. Helped by Parliamentary reform and especially the coming of the secret ballot in 1872, Wales became a country dominated by Liberal politicians and, when the Liberal Party was in power, a significant force in British politics. This influence resulted from the 1880s in legislation which was both radical and specifically Welsh.

Much of the dynamic for the Liberal achievement emanated from its alliance, even identity, with religious Nonconformity. As Dr Christopher Turner explains, it was Nonconformist denominations, Calvinistic and Wesleyan Methodist, Congregationalist (Independent) and Baptist, which dominated Welsh religious and, to a marked degree, political life. Yet conventional Liberalism tended hardly to touch some of the most profound social problems produced by industrialization.

The next two essays, by Dr David Howell and Dr David Jones, examine movements of popular protest in Wales, two of which, Rebecca and Scotch Cattle, were notable for their use of elaborate disguises. The Rebecca Riots were more firmly rooted in Wales's rural past than the Scotch Cattle, though both were linked with Chartism. The lot of the small tenant farmers of south-west Wales led to violent protest against oppression. The symbol of this oppression became the toll-gates. Toll-gates were erected at frequent intervals along the roads and farmers had to pay for each animal or each load they ushered through. Their response, in the 1840s, was to break down the gates. They did so in a variety of colourful disguises under the leadership of a man dressed in a woman's clothing and always addressed as Rebecca. The use of the name Rebecca may well have been derived from a reference in the Bible to Rebecca and her descendants inheriting the gates of their enemies. The disguising of the protesters' identity, a feature of the Scotch Cattle and the Rebecca movements, ties both in with the communal direct action of previous centuries.

The complications of the inter-relationship of economic, social and political changes are highlighted in protest in north Wales in the second half of the nineteenth century. In rural Wales, there was opposition, once more with both parliamentary and physical manifestations, against the tithes which hard-pressed farmers had to pay to an alien established church, the Church of England, and against the pressure on land which led to landlords raising rents. Symptoms of change and continuity were even more evident in the quarrying districts of north Wales where the Welsh-speaking, Nonconformist craftsmen, who mined and quarried slate, became locked in sporadic dispute from the 1860s to 1903 with the landlords of the old order who were, as quarry owners, fully-fledged capitalist proprietors. These confrontations encapsulated a rural and urban Wales, a Welsh-speaking and anglicized Wales, a nation of capital and labour wrought from the Industrial Revolution and a Wales where both Liberal and socialist concerns loomed large, at least for the moment.

At one level *People and Protest: Wales 1815–1880* is simply a book about the history of Wales at a time when a number of fundamental changes were taking place, and about the ways in which historians interpret that period. However, the series of which this volume is a part has been designed to serve a number of functions for anyone who is formally or informally engaged in a study of Welsh history. Those studying with a tutor, for instance extra-mural, university or sixth-form students, will find that it is a resource which will form a basis for, or enhance, a broader study of Welsh history. Those who are studying in a more remote location, far from formal classes in Welsh history, will find that the contents of the book are so ordered as to guide them through a course of study similar, but not analogous, to the methods which have proved successful in continuing education programmes of the Open University. The main feature of this method is that it attempts to combine a programmatic approach with something more flexible and open-ended.

Central to this book are Sections A to F which contain three different but closely related and interlinked types of material. Each of the six essays is written on a clearly-defined topic. Each essay is immediately followed by a collection of source material which is the basis of the evidence for the essay. Within each essay reference is made to a particular source document by the inclusion of a reference number in the essay text; this reference number is also placed in the left hand margin of the essay.

The sources section of each topic is followed by a section called 'Debating the Evidence'. The primary purpose here is to highlight the special features, weaknesses and strengths of each collection of sources and to question the way in which the author of the essay has used them. It is worth pointing out that we have not attempted here simply to act as *agents provocateurs*, setting up a series of artificial controversies which can be comfortably demolished. The purpose is to raise the sorts of questions which essayists themselves probably addressed before they employed these sources. In doing this we hope to expose the types of issues that the historian has to deal with. The 'Debating the Evidence' sections pose a number of questions about the sources. They neither provide model answers nor neatly tie up all of the loose ends concerning each source. The discipline of history does not allow that approach. If it did, there would be no need for a book of this type. The 'discussions' which round off each section simply put forward a number of ideas which will cause readers to consider and reconsider the issues which have been raised. The purpose is to breed the kind of healthy scepticism about historical sources which underlies the method of approach of the professional historian.

Other parts of the book support these central sections. The Introduction poses basic problems about the difficulties of coping with historical sources, points which are consolidated in the 'Debating the Evidence' sections. The intention of the opening essay, *People and Protest 1815–1880*, is to outline the principal changes which took place in Wales during this period and to hint at the issues that motivated those changes.

At the end of the book is a glossary which explains briefly a number of the more technical terms and concepts arising out of the essays/documents collection. Although a glossary is properly a list of explanations of words and terms, we have additionally included brief details of persons who are prominent in the essay and document material. Words *italicized* (thus) in the text will normally be explained in the glossary.

Readers will, of course, decide how best to profit from the different constituent elements in the book. The first two chapters should certainly be read first, as these provide a context for the rest of the book. It is also important to read the six essays (with or without reference to the source collections) before reading the 'Debating the Evidence' sections. It is necessary to have this broad framework for examining and re-examining the collections of sources. The 'Debating the Evidence' sections refer both forward and back to various sources on the assumption that you have familiarized yourself with the material in this way.

The open-ended nature of the book serves to highlight the extent to which it has been our intention to do no more than *contribute* to an understanding of Welsh history. Different editors would have chosen different topics. The essays here should be seen within the framework of a much wider range of writings which over the past few decades has become available. The greatest success which a book like this can meet with is that it imparts to its readers an insatiable desire to know more about Welsh history and to do so from a standpoint which is constantly and intelligently questioning the ways in which historians provide that knowledge.

Acknowledgements

The development of the Welsh History and its Sources project was made possible by the support of the Secretary of State for Wales and I am happy to have made formal acknowledgement to the Secretary of State and individuals connected with the project elsewhere in this book.

Funding from the Open University made possible the development of the initial ideas that were eventually nurtured by a Welsh Office grant. The assistance of various individuals and departments of the Open University has been frequently and freely given. In particular, my colleagues at the Open University in Wales, where the project was based, have been constantly helpful. Julia Williams, secretary to the Arts Faculty of the Open University in Wales, acted as secretary to the project. As well as word processing the texts for the entire series she was immensely efficient in the administration of the project.

University College, Swansea, were kind enough to allow the part secondment of Dr Gareth Elwyn Jones to work on the project. Without him the project would not have progressed beyond being an idea as I have relied entirely on his widely respected expertise for overseeing the academic content of the series.

Diverse contributions have enhanced the effectiveness of the material. John Hunt of the Open University drew the maps and diagrams, often from a jumble of data and instructions. Photographic research and administration was done by Rhodri Morgan. Annette Musker compiled the Index. Copyright administration of textual material was done by Richard McCracken. Anne Howells of the University of Wales Press copy-edited the series and made many useful suggestions for improvement. I am grateful to Dr D.A.T. Thomas of the Open University in Wales for advice on and translation of certain Welsh language passages.

My major debt of gratitude is to the contributors, each of whom was asked to write to a prescribed topic, format, word length and submission date. Each fulfilled the brief with absolute accuracy, punctuality and co-operation. The format was prescribed by me. Any shortcomings that remain can be put down to that prescription and to the consequences that emanated from it.

TREVOR HERBERT
Cardiff
March 1987

Introduction

The essays contained in this book have been written not only by specialist historians, but also by specialists in the particular topic on which they have written. They are authorities on their subject and they make pertinent, informed and professional observations. Each essay is an important contribution to the historiography of Wales.

As specialists they know the sources for their topics intimately. They have included extracts from a cross-section of these sources to indicate on what evidence they base the generalizations and conclusions in their essays. We hope that the essays will interest you and that the documents will bring you into contact with kinds of primary sources which you may not have encountered before. Historians face a variety of problems when they consult source material and face even more difficulties when they have to synthesize the material collected into a coherent narrative and analysis of the events they are describing. In doing so the best historians make mistakes. Sometimes these are trivial (or not so trivial!) errors of fact. You may even spot factual discrepancies between information given in the various essays and the documents in this book.

At the end of each essay/sources section there is a short discussion section. By the time you reach it you will have read the essay and the sources on which the essay is based.

The discussion section is concerned with problems of interpretation. It is an attempt to conduct a debate with the author about the way in which the essay relates to the sources. This is partly achieved by asking pertinent questions about the nature of the sources. The intention is that you are stimulated to think about the validity of the exercise of writing history and the methodology of the study of history which is essentially what distinguishes it from other disciplines. The dialogue is a complex one and the questions posed do not, generally, have any 'right' answers.

But they do have some answers which make more sense than others. We feel that the historians who have written the essays have provided answers which are reasonable. But historians are not infallible, however eminent they may be. Their conclusions are open to debate and discussion, as, for that matter, is their whole procedure of working. As you work through the discussion and questions you will notice that there is specific cross-referencing to the relevant section of the essay (or essays) and to documents. It is important that you use these cross-references since the success of the exercise depends vitally on taking into account the relationship between the primary source material and what the historian makes of it.

At the heart of the historian's task is the search for and subsequent use of evidence, much of it of the sort you will encounter here. The crucial distinction in the nature of this evidence is that between primary and secondary sources. There is no completely watertight definition of what constitutes a primary source but a reasonable working definition would be that primary sources consist of material which came into existence during the particular period which the historian is researching, while secondary sources came into existence after that period. Another important point is that the extent to which a source can be regarded as primary or secondary relies as much on the topic of research as it does on the date of that source.

For example, David Jones, in his essay on the Scotch Cattle and Chartism, refers, in his second paragraph, to the eminent Welsh historian, the late Professor David Williams and remarks that Williams was saddened by these episodes. This viewpoint emerges in David Williams's pioneering work on Chartism, *John Frost: A Study in Chartism*, published in 1939. The date indicates that this book is a secondary source for the present-day historian studying Chartism, since it was written and published roughly one hundred years after the events analysed in it. However, if Dr Jones were asking a different question from the one which is the subject of the essay, Williams's book might fall into the category of primary source. For example, if Dr Jones were to develop the question implicit in the comment in his essay, that is, to question the way in which historians have looked at and written about Chartism from, say, 1840 to 1940, then David Williams's book would be a primary source and it would provide us, unwittingly, with particularly enlightening information as to the way a fine historian's views on Chartism tell us much about his own views of his country and his society.

The interpretation of historical sources is extremely complex. It was once believed by highly reputable historians that if they mastered all the sources they could write 'true' history. There is at least one eminent historian who argues this now. You might like to consider on which side of the debate you stand at the moment.

Most historians would argue that this is impossible. Because we are removed from the time and place of the event, we are influenced by prejudices of nationality, religion or politics. However, there is some compensation for this because we know, usually, what the results were of actions which occurred during the period of a given topic and this benefit of hindsight is enormously useful in trying to analyse the interplay of various factors in a situation and their influence on subsequent events. As you read the essays and documents in this collection, consider the degree of objectivity and subjectivity displayed by the authors. To do this you will need to consider what you would like to know about the authors before coming to a decision and how far the authors are entitled to their own interpretations. Of course, you, too, may come to the material with your own prejudices.

There is a similar pattern of presentation for each essay and its related documents. There are specific questions involving comprehension, evaluation, interpretation and synthesis, with synthesis, arguably, the highest level of the skills. However, there can be no rigid demarcation of historical skills such as interpretation and synthesis and some questions will overlap the various categories. Neither is there a standard form of 'answer', as the discussions demonstrate. What the questions do provide is guidance for a structured pattern of study which will enhance your understanding of the essays and documents.

Above all, there is dialogue and discussion about the way in which each historian has handled the complexities of writing about and interpreting the past. That such interpretation is as skilled, informed and mature as is conceivably possible is essential to our well-being as a society. In that these books are about the history of Wales they contribute fundamentally to that end. That vitality depends on debate, analytical, informed, structured debate. It is the purpose of this book to stimulate your involvement in that debate in a more structured way than has been attempted before in the study of the history of Wales.

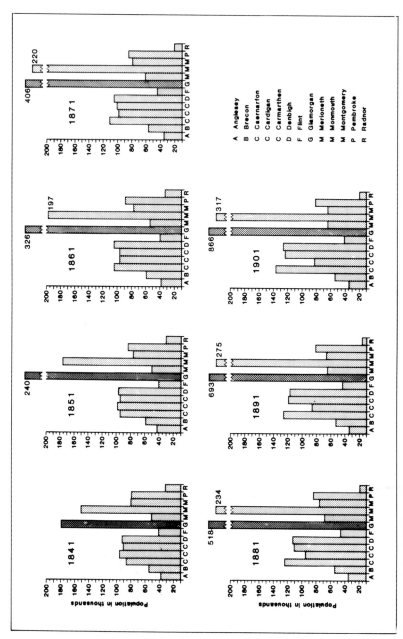

County populations in Wales as shown by census returns.

Timechart

Wales		Other Significant Events

THE LEFT-HAND COLUMN CONTAINS ITEMS WHICH ARE SPECIFIC TO WALES OR WHICH HAD A PARTICULAR IMPORTANCE FOR WALES. THE RIGHT-HAND COLUMN LISTS SOME OF THE MORE SIGNIFICANT CONTEMPORARY EVENTS.

Wales		Other Significant Events
	1799/ 1800	Combination Acts passed.
	1815	Corn Law introduced.
Ironworkers strike in south Wales and riots at Merthyr Tydfil.	**1816**	
Riots at Carmarthen during food shortages.	**1818**	
	1819	Peterloo 'massacre'.
Riots by lead miners at Halkyn. Colliers' strike in Monmouthshire. First appearance of Scotch Cattle.	**1822**	
	1824	Repeal of the Combination Act which had forbidden trade unions.
Dispute at Penrhyn Quarries	**1825**	Stockton and Darlington railway opened.

Repeal of Test and Corporations Act which had disqualified Nonconformists.	**1828**	
Enclosure disturbances at Llanddulas.	**1829**	Peel's Metropolitan Police Act creates first uniformed force in Britain.
First cholera epidemic in Wales. Reform 'crisis'. Merthyr Rising followed by hanging of Dic Penderyn. Anti-Truck Act passed.	**1831**	Lord John Russell introduces first Reform Bill — resigns after its defeat.
Parliamentary Reform Act passed. Religious revival.	**1832**	First Reform Act.
Poor Law Amendment Act passed.	**1834**	Tolpuddle Martyrs transported.
Arrest and trial of Scotch Cattle.	**1835**	Municipal Corporations Act.
Tithe Commutation Act passed.	**1836**	
First Working Men's Association formed at Carmarthen.	**1837**	Queen Victoria succeeds to throne.
Publication of People's Charter.	**1838**	Anti-Corn Law League founded.
Chartist disturbances at Llanidloes. Chartist march on Newport. First Rebecca attacks.	**1839**	Chartist riots in Birmingham.
Renewal of Rebecca attacks. Chartist revival and strike in south Wales.	**1842**	
Rebecca at its height.	**1843**	

Formation of Liberation Society. Turnpike Trusts Act reforms these bodies.	1844	
	1845–51	Irish Famine.
	1846	Repeal of the Corn Laws.
Commission on Education in Wales ('Blue Books'). Cholera epidemic.	1847	
Public Health Act allows Local Boards of Health to be created. Chartist revival.	1848	Third of Chartist petitions presented to Parliament. Year of revolutions in Europe.
Religious revival.	1849	
Strike of Holywell copper workers.	1850	
Census of Religious Worship.	1851	The Great Exhibition.
Strike of Llanddulas copper workers. Chartist revival.	1853	
	1854–6	Crimean War.
	1855	Tax on newspapers repealed.
Law makes it compulsory for all counties and boroughs to have police force. Disturbances at Talargoch lead mines.	1856	
Political evictions in Merionethshire following General Election. Religious revival. *Baner ac Amserau Cymru* started by Thomas Gee.	1859	

	1861–5	American Civil War.
National Reform Union formed to campaign for household suffrage.	**1864**	
First attempt to form trade union at Penrhyn Quarry.	**1865**	Irish Church Act disestablished the 'Anglican' church in Ireland. Salvation Army founded by William Booth.
National Reform League founded to campaign for manhood suffrage and secret ballot.	**1866**	
Second Reform Act enfranchises working-class householders in towns.	**1867**	
Liberal victories in Wales in General Election.	**1868**	National Federation of trade unions starts meeting annually.
Mold Riots.	**1869**	
	1870–1	Franco-Prussian War.
	1870	Education Act.
Ballot Act introduces secret ballot.	**1872**	
	1874–6	Major social reforms by Disraeli's government.
North Wales Quarrymen's Union formed.	**1874**	
	1875	Public Health Act.
	1878	Congress of Berlin.
	1879	Irish National Land League founded.
	1880–1	First Boer War.

	1880	Education Act in effect makes education compulsory for five to ten year olds.
Sunday Closing (Wales) Act.	**1881**	
Reform Act enfranchises working-class householders in countryside.	**1884**	
Strikes at Llanddulas and Llanberis.	**1885**	
Welsh Land League formed. Beginning of 'Tithe War' in north Wales.	**1886**	

Wales, showing the pre-1974 county boundaries.

People and Protest: Wales 1815–1880

IEUAN GWYNEDD JONES

The years between about 1820 and 1895 were the most momentous in the history of modern Wales. It was during that short period — the lifespan of an oldish person as the expectation of life was then measured — that the social consequences of the first stage of the industrialization of Wales became apparent, and it was in that period that those consequences would be fully worked out in the transformation of Welsh society. It was a time of great contradictions. Violence was never far from the surface, but saintly men and women were among the most admired characters of the age. Huge numbers of people took part in great demonstrations to show their solidarity and in riots to express their rage: but they also worshipped together in great congregations and the most prestigious buildings in the settlements where they lived were chapels and places of worship. It was a period full of political movement and energy. It began with *Radicalism*, passed through *Chartism*, and quickly learned the doctrines and techniques of representative democracy. It began with attempts among the working classes to discipline themselves in accordance with their own distinct moralities, and having achieved a mature understanding of trade *unionism* ended the period with working-class organizations based on the idea not of confrontation but on a kind of consensus. It was a period full of cultural paradoxes. The formal religion of the Church of England was largely rejected and unofficial types of religious worship, the religions of the oppressed and the rejected, flourished in its stead. It was also the time when Welsh, the ancient language of the people, its medium for the expression and transmission of their high culture, began its slow retreat in the face of the inexorable advance of the English language.

The new society was growing rapidly in numbers. It doubled in the period between 1821 and 1881, growing from around 800,000, itself a huge increase since the middle of the eighteenth century, to just over 1,500,000. It was a very young population with a large dependent population of small children who had to be socialized into working for their livings at very tender ages, in town and country alike. It was also a population which was being radically redistributed about the country in response to the irresistible duality of rural over-population and the demands of the new industries for a steady supply of labour.

Most evident, though least understood, was the growth of new kinds of communities. Ancient seaports, like Swansea and Newport, Cardiff and Caernarfon, had already expanded as the new means of communication — tramways, canals, railways — knit them into the economy of copper, iron, coal and slates. Old towns, like Neath and Flint, outside which industries had developed, grew suburbs and began that apparently inevitable process of social segregation whereby the salubrious and fashionable quarters moved away, and were kept distant, from the crowded working-class areas. But most alarming was the expansion of the 'mining and manufactory districts', those amorphous working-class industrial settlements which appeared suddenly in rural surroundings or on uninhabited moorland, filling valleys with collier communities bereft of institutions of government, having apparently no centres of civilization beyond their chapels, *Sunday Schools* and *friendly societies.* Many of these on the coalfields of south and north Wales grew faster even than the old iron towns had grown, but unlike them they seemed to be impermanent, the temporary habitations of a rootless people. They were 'towns of an adventitious character', 'condensations of people' filled, it was believed, with a sensual and ignorant people, disaffected towards the state and hostile towards their employers. So the industrial areas filled with people until by 1881 more than half the total population of Wales lived in Glamorgan, Monmouthshire and the eastern side of Carmarthenshire. More than one-third of the population of Merioneth lived in Blaenau Ffestiniog. Wales had become an urban country and many of its rural districts, wherever there was coal, or iron, or slates, had assumed the character of towns.

This redistribution of a constantly growing population had profound effects on the rural areas, for it was they who were providing people for the new industrial areas. This had been the case from the earliest days of industrialization: Merthyr Tydfil and the other iron towns at the heads of the valleys had been peopled by migrants from adjacent parts of the counties concerned and from over the county borders. As the demands for labour grew so they came from more distant parts, from south-west and mid-Wales. In this period only industrializing counties gained population, and all counties, with the notable exception of Glamorgan, suffered a net loss by out-migration. The counties with least industry were the ones to be soonest depopulated.

Almost certainly the sanitary conditions of rural and urban areas deteriorated for the first thirty or forty years of our period. The death rate for the country as a whole in the 1850s was around 22 per 1,000 per annum. That was an average figure which concealed wide variations: in small rural towns and in the new industrial districts it could be as high as 30 per 1,000. Infant mortality was horrifyingly high: in Merthyr Tydfil in the decade 1851–60 it was 184 per 1,000 live births. No-one can tell how many still-births there were or how many births went unrecorded.

These high levels of mortality — in some towns almost as high as in the great industrial cities of England — were undoubtedly related to bad sanitary conditions, poor housing and crowded conditions, malnutrition, insufficient clothing, excessive labour in unhealthy conditions, and ignorance. It is a myth that country people, least of all the farm labourers, were better housed, better fed, and healthier. Like the inhabitants of the crowded towns they were subject to the ravages of endemic killer diseases, to frequent epidemics of contagious and infectious diseases against which most people were unprotected, and to wasting diseases such as tuberculosis. It is probable that the people who fled to the towns from the grinding poverty of the countryside brought debilitating diseases with them and that their low physical condition made them an easy prey to the characteristic diseases and hazards of the towns. Disease does not discriminate between social classes, as the cholera epidemics of the time demonstrated: but some of the main constituents of social class, such as higher incomes, better housing, diet, clothing, and education helped in some measure to defend the better off in town and country from the worst ravages of disease. Not until the Public Health Legislation of the 1840s and 1850s had been made obligatory on all local authorities, including the supply of clean water, better sanitation, and improved medical services, did conditions change for the better. In the Welsh valleys it may very well have been the case that the improvements following the *Public Health Act of 1872* and the reorganization of local government of the same time were negated by the headlong population growth of the last decades of the century.

Throughout the period, and increasingly as industrialization continued in its irregular progress of boom and bust, the inequalities in society became more pronounced. Undoubtedly it was the employment and wealth generated by industry that enabled the vast bulk of Welsh people to remain in the land, if not in the locality, of their birth: the alternative would have been the Irish experience of mass migration overseas during the Great Famine and after. Welsh peasants in the south-west were also becoming over-dependent on the potato as a staple crop. But industrialization also widened the social gulf between rich and poor. Townscapes and building styles reflected these differences, the beneficiaries of capitalism distancing themselves from its victims, the poor who, whether in their pre-migratory rural days or in the towns in which they found themselves, had borne and continued to bear the brunt of the pressures of population and food. Immense fortunes were being made in industry and commerce — Wales had its millionaires — but the spending of private fortunes on public causes was not one of the characteristic features of their life-style; and the towns and industrial villages of north and south Wales reflected not the riches of the industrialists but the relative poverty and deprivation of the workforce.

Evidence of the same kind of social distancing was to be found in the countryside. The conspicuous consumption of estate owners, especially of the small and medium-sized owners whose tastes were in inverse relation to their incomes, the frantic and extravagant rebuilding of the old *plastai* and mansions and the pursuit of aristocratic styles of living were often perceived to be at the expense of the rural poor. The Welsh farm labourer, enigmatically silent in his hovel, and the small tenant farmer scraping a living out of land that would never be his own, were both held in the vice of economic dependence and social inferiority. The problem of the rural poor at the gate of the rich was as acute as that of the pauperized masses in the towns.

Poverty, something experienced only by the lower classes, but defined in legislation by the ruling classes, was the major problem of the age. At the beginning of our period it was being dealt with by a kind of *ad hoc* combination of private charity and public welfare. After the *Poor Law Amendment Act* of 1834, which established a strict, uniform and centrally enforceable system of relief based on workhouses serving unions of parishes, it seemed to those who suffered that poverty had come to be regarded more as an offence than a misfortune by those who administered the law, and not to sink into the state of complete dependency and degradation of the pauper class became a prime aim of the respectable poor. In the bitter 1840s, when agricultural distress was deepest, workhouses came under attack and troops were needed to protect them as in south-west Wales in 1843.

These were the social conditions, these the pressures, which underlay the movements of popular protest discussed in the essays that follow. Many were clearly related to economic fluctuations, agricultural depression, slumps in the iron trade and worsening economic conditions generally. But they could also be aroused by perceptions or feelings on the part of groups or of whole communities that their standard of living was declining in conditions of relative plenty, that they were being exploited or treated unfairly by those in authority. Miners in Merthyr in the early 1850s who had been ready to work for less during depression resented the refusal of the masters to pay more for their labour now that trade had improved. Invariably in such cases disturbances were justified on grounds of justice and fair play. Historians have pointed out that many popular disturbances in England were defensive in character and deeply conservative in that they appealed to community values and moral codes which were believed to govern the relations between different groups in society. Thus custom and a community's sense of what was right and proper determined the common reaction to the grievances complained of. Ritual, like the *ceffyl pren* (wooden horse) described by Dr Jones or the wearing of women's garments by the Rebecca rioters described by Dr Howell, was characteristic of these pre-industrial protests and disturbances. This was why they were feared by the authorities: they signified a widespread and effective rejection of conventional codes of behaviour, and were most dangerous when they were most secret in their operation.

Of great significance in the development of Welsh society during this period was the diminution after the 1850s both in intensity, frequency and geographical spread of these forms of protest and the shift to more peaceful and constitutional forms. Some historians have attributed this to improvements in the economic climate, but it is necessary to bear in mind that the economy, like the weather, fluctuated widely from time to time and from place to place: it is extremely doubtful that the conditions of life of peasants in south-west Wales were significantly better in the mid-1860s than they had been twenty years earlier. It would be perverse to infer improved conditions from the absence of militancy. In the industrial areas the move to trade unions was consciously a move away from the endemic and particularized violence of the beginning of our period to more openly organized, rational, restrained and institutional-ized forms of conflict. In an astonishingly short period of time the industrial workers of north and south Wales had created more or less permanent and very mature trade unions, in which violent protest was the exception and controlled, massive demonstrations the norm. The horns of the *Scotch Cattle* were still heard, but less frequently and to less effect.

Behind this were two developments of a fundamental kind, religion and politics. It must never be forgotten that the massive growth of *Nonconformity* in Wales was itself the most characteristic protest movement of the time. If, as was probably the case, disturbances and protests coincided with years of acute social tension, so also did the growth of the *Nonconformist* denominations. By the 1850s patterns of adherence had been firmly established and the Welsh people moved into the middle decades of the century with immensely powerful, well integrated and pacific religious denominations as their most character-istic creation and with a primary claim on the loyalty of the common people. The moral and cultural values of religion made for debate rather than conflict, for consensus rather than confrontation, and for respect for legality and the constitution in the pursuit of political ends. Thus, religion reinforced the old *Chartist* drive for constitutional reform. By the 1860s the chapels of most of the denominations had become potential political centres devoted to teaching peaceful ways of protest, relying on the pulpit and platform and schoolroom, supporting the press and looking towards parliament for redress of grievances of all kinds. Violent forms of protest did not cease, but they were less in evidence at the end of the period than at the beginning. The people had been politicized.

The Urbanization of Welsh Society

NEIL EVANS

Towns are concentrated slices of a society. The number and kinds of towns display much of the underlying social reality. In nineteenth-century Wales the changes in the nature, distribution and significance of towns are a key to understanding the transformation that took place under the impact of industrialization. As Wales industrialized it became urbanized too; that is the proportion of its population living in towns increased, and by 1890 this was much greater than the rural population.

The scattered rural population of pre-industrial Wales had not needed, nor been able to support, large or numerous towns. Visiting travellers were usually unimpressed by the urban life they saw and they often portrayed urban decay rather than urban growth. The Reverend Richard Warner, passing through Brecon in 1797, observed, 'Like most other towns in Wales, this place is interesting rather from what it has been, than on account of what it now is' (A.1). Castle towns planted for conquest in the Middle Ages had not always flourished — Harlech found little trade in the fastness of Ardudwy and ceased to be the county town of Merioneth. It was eclipsed by Dolgellau, a market town and manufacturing centre which grew from the Tudor period onwards, and was better adapted to the needs of the surrounding society. Caernarfon was a castle town which found a role in the surrounding society as a market and centre of administration. These three towns in Gwynedd symbolize the urban pattern of eighteenth-century Wales. None was large; one was a castle town which had been nurtured in Welsh soil, another was one which had withered in stony soil

A.1

7

and the third was an unplanned native growth. At the centre of many towns, such as Brecon and Caernarfon, were the *plasau* of the gentry for whom town life held growing attractions for at least part of the year. Tenby drew the Pembrokeshire gentry in the summer and Haverfordwest with its balls, dinners, card games and plays was the winter attraction. Perhaps it was fitting that in a society where land was the key source of wealth that even the towns should have a strong presence of rural landlords.

By the end of the nineteenth century industry, not land, was the pulse of Wales. Towns grew and were transformed in the process of change. The relationship between industrialization and urbanization is not an inevitable nor a necessary one. Much of the industrial production of eighteenth-century Wales was comfortably housed in farm houses and weaving sheds in rural areas, requiring only small towns to co-ordinate production and marketing. Nor do towns invariably become industrial centres — transport, marketing and professional services can and do sustain them. Eighteenth-century Wales looked across the border for the urban functions which it was unable to provide for itself. None of the border towns which played significant roles was primarily industrial in origin. In the course of the nineteenth century, however, the relationship between industry and towns became so close that now we tend to regard the words as being interchangeable. Yet even in the nineteenth century, when population tended to crowd into the coalfields, the relationship was not as simple and congruent as it at first appears.

Industry was slow to weave its urban magic. At the taking of the first census in 1801 there was no town of more than ten thousand people in Wales and only four of more than five thousand. Merthyr Tydfil was the largest with 7,705 in encampments around the booming ironworks of the vast upland parish (A.2, A.3, A.4). It had no obvious centre but was the capital of a larger ironworking district which stretched across the heads of the valleys of eastern south Wales. Once the population of Wales had been fairly evenly spread and concentrated only where the soil was rich. By 1880 it was the proximity of coal which most affected the density of population. Wales had much leeway to make up. In the eighteenth century it

A.2
A.3
A.4

had been perhaps the least urbanized part of Britain and for much of the following hundred years it lagged behind the overall level of Britain, yet by 1880 it was clearly an area of concentrated population. In 1851 under 20 per cent of the population lived in towns of over 5,000 people; in 1891 just under 50 per cent; and by 1911 nearly 60 per cent. In 1901 there were 28 towns of more than 10,000 people and 55 of more than 5,000. Cardiff, the largest town since 1871 and with 182,259 people in 1911, capped an urban civilization with white palaces springing up in the greenery of Cathays Park. It was the premier coal-exporting and tramp-shipping port in the world and second only to London in the volume of cargo it cleared.

Out of the shifting relationship between industry and the towns it helped generate, it was Cardiff, a transport and service centre with only a small industrial base, which emerged at the top of the pile. Coal concentrated people but it was a town offset from the coalfield which benefitted most from the process. This is not a paradox when properly understood, but it needs explanation. Industry directly created many settlements, but the people assembled had needs other than jobs. Feeding them, clothing them, entertaining them, transporting their product and attending to the needs of commerce created needs for urban facilities which went beyond the simple requirements of housing a workforce. The historians J.L. and Barbara Hammond once described nineteenth-century towns as the 'barracks of the new industrial civilization', but, in reality, far more than dormitories were created.

Many different kinds of towns settled into the Welsh landscape in the nineteenth century. The ironworks settlements at the head of the eastern valleys were the first and most fearsome. Most were unplanned and only slowly acquired the new forms of government necessary for a town. Only rising *poor rates* persuaded the ironmasters to look out from the works in Merthyr towards the vestry which served as its government A.2 (A.2, A.3, A.4). In the mid-century it still lacked suitable means A.3 to cope with its growth and even after the creation of a local A.4 Board of Health in 1850 progress was slow because the dominating power of the rates-conscious ironmasters blocked the reforming aspirations of the tiny middle class of lawyers, shopkeepers and merchants. The heads-of-the-valleys area held 150,000 people by the fourth decade of the nineteenth century, and shops and services began to make them more complex and diverse. This was less true of the primitive coal camps to the south. Amenities were even fewer and the middle class not small but miniscule. The small capital needed to sink the pits did not produce the towering figures and occasional paternalists of the northern part of the 'Black Domain' of industrial south Wales. Small masters fought for their own existence in a savagely competitive market and here *laissez-faire* capitalism reached its nadir. Smaller populations and more rural settings meant they were healthier than the still unsewered and undrained towns of the north but social life was more savage.

As the head of the octopus grew in the coalfield, so its tentacles of trade and service reached out and enlarged the towns on its edges. Cardiff, a decayed castle town serving mainly as a port and market for the Vale of Glamorgan with a village-like population of 1,870 in 1801 grew tenfold to reach 18,351 in 1851 mainly because of the iron it exported from Merthyr. The Glamorgan canal, opened in 1794, was its lifeline. To the north, Brecon also found there were side-effects to industrial growth. Two canals and a tramroad gave it good links with the coalfield and helped make it an assembly point for food gathered on the rich fields of Herefordshire as well as south Powys. Professional services, retailing, handicraft workers and legal services expanded. In 1831, 55 per cent of men over twenty years of age worked in retailing and services. The barracks erected in 1805 also reflected the impact of the turbulent coalfield to the south. In the years 1801 to 1851 Brecon's population more than doubled, industrial development nearby helping it to keep pace with the average national trend.

Swansea in the west of the coalfield grew more than threefold in the equivalent period, because it had many more functions to perform. Its historical role as a bridge point and market centre where the rich Gower peninsula joined the less fertile upland Glamorgan had been supplemented by a developing role as a sea-bathing resort in the eighteenth century. Coal exports, copper and lead smelting won a head-on confrontation with tourism. A pall of copper smoke took away the tang of the sea air, and industry rather than tourists sustained its growth in the nineteenth century.

Similar patterns were evident over much of the rest of Wales, if we change the names of the settlements and scale down the absolute levels of population growth. The slate industry produced its equivalent of the heads-of-the-valleys towns in Bethesda and Llanberis which sprang up around single industrial enterprises, industrial fiefs of landowning slate-barons. Bethesda took its name from its first chapel, though subsequent assertions of *Nonconformist* independence were to prove more difficult. The Penrhyn estate built a model village at Llandygái, but on the neighbouring Cefnfaes estate controls were absent and houses were built 'with great contempt for regularity, wherever a patch of tolerably level ground could be found facing any point of the compass the builder might fancy'. In the later-developing areas of Nantlle and Ffestiniog — both took off in the 1830s — there were numerous smaller concerns and they never had such tight yokes of *Tory*, Church of England landlordism, for their newly-rich capitalists had much in common in politics and religion with their workforce. None of the slate towns became large, though their rates of growth were sometimes spectacular. By 1881 Ffestiniog had 11,274 people and was more or less at the peak of its development; Bethesda had 7,739 people in 1871 (almost the same as Merthyr at the turn of the century) but its most rapid period of growth was already behind it. Its population had grown by 61.2 per cent in the decade 1831–41, but by only 56.6 per cent in the three decades from 1841 to 1871. Slate required its ports and services too and they duly developed. The old towns of Bangor and Caernarfon swelled with new prosperity and new ones like Porthmadog and Port Dinorwic bounded up to match them. The building of ships to transport the slate developed in many Gwynedd ports and a world-wide trade, not confined to slate, grew out of this. Industry always had a multiplier effect on urbanization.

The removal of coal export duties in the 1840s and the coming of mining technology which permitted shafts to be driven deep enough to reach the well-buried steam coal of the central portions of the south Wales coalfield allowed communities similar to Blaenau Ffestiniog to grow elsewhere. Iron made Aberdare an outlier of Merthyr but steam coal enabled it to challenge for supremacy. It had its coal-owning dynasties, but Thomas Powell was never really a rival to Guest and Crawshay. The shared *Nonconformist* background between coalowner and collier allowed a liberal Welsh language press to flourish there. Where Aberdare pointed, Rhondda followed; the line of shafts and settlements steadily pushing up the valleys from Pontypridd until in 1907 it was observed that 'The industrial townships of this valley appear to be inseparably connected in one continuous series of streets from the head of the vale to Pontypridd.' Deep mines and their large workforces gave them a different aspect from the tiny encampments of the southern Black Domain. Rhondda's transformation from tourist spot to black spot was sudden and dramatic. In the 1850s 'with the exception of a village here and there and a few farmhouses and homesteads, there was nothing to interfere with its natural beauty', and there were only about two thousand people in the area. In 1901 there were 113,735 people, more than in most of the counties of Wales. The new mix of population and narrow treeless valleys was not an aesthetic success. Gwyn Thomas observed pungently, 'Society and nature have come together to achieve some amazing patterns, and they should be told not to do it again.'

Other colliery districts followed similar, if rather less spectacular, paths. In north-east Wales the old market and gentry centre of Wrexham was bloated by the trade it sucked in from its garland of colliery villages. The north-east Wales coalfield developed a wider array of small industrial towns than did south Wales. Flint, an old castle town became a prime centre of lead smelting, Ruabon made bricks and Bersham, steel. Along the north Wales coast there developed a series of seaside resorts. Prestatyn, Rhyl, Colwyn Bay and Llandudno were on an ascending scale of planning and social class. Llandudno, carefully developed by the Mostyn estate, attracted the *bourgeoisie* of Lancashire; bank holidays, *wakes weeks* and shorter distances attracted an emerging *proletariat* to the less elevated resorts (A.5). Prosperous tourists were also penetrating to other Welsh coastal towns by the mid-century. Aberystwyth had its centre of gravity tipped from its old market cross in the vicinity

A.5

of its castle to the new Promenade which announced its emerging role. Barmouth developed new canyon-like streets of guest houses and shops near its sea-front once the Cambrian Coast Railway made it accessible in the 1860s.

In south Wales resorts were slower to develop; Penarth catered for a middle-class clientele. Once it was clear that its coal-exporting days were done in the 1880s, Porthcawl began to be developed by the Maesteg ironmasters, the Brogdens. Barry Island only came into its own after the opening of the dock in 1889. In south Wales miners' families lacked the female earnings which existed in, and which benefited, the north Wales resorts. Nor did they win for themselves the leisure that their Lancashire compatriots did.

Resorts were the product of an industrial society, the result of the unequally distributed and slowly spreading leisure time and spending power which Victorian prosperity generated. Industry's effect on the urban pattern was fundamental but never simple; it impinged on an existing distribution of towns and the reach of its transformation was a long one, far beyond production into distribution, exchange and leisure. It made counting houses and playgrounds as well as workshops and dormitories. Rapid growth rates were characteristic of many Welsh towns and the inadequate framework of government ensured that this was a recipe for social and environmental crisis.

The most pressing problem was public health. The sanitary arrangements of the early industrial towns did not differ in any way from those of the countryside, but practices which were tolerable if only a few houses clustered together, and unpleasant in villages and small towns, became a menace to survival amidst a teeming population (A.6, A.7, A.8, A.9). Typhus and other zymotic diseases (diseases caused and spread by germs) were endemic killers in the towns, particularly in the cruel tithe of young children they took each summer. Yet it was the dramatic epidemics of Asiatic cholera which prompted action. Cholera's advance across Europe would be rumoured for weeks, even months. When it arrived it made a sudden and dramatic carnage and the manner of death was particularly horrible. Overall it killed fewer people than typhus, but it was a drama which

A.6
A.7
A.8
A.9

persuaded others to act. In the wake of the first epidemic of
1831–32 the temporary public health measures of that time were
allowed to lapse. In the 1840s the first major investigations of
sanitary conditions in towns were made. One of these commented, 'Merthyr Tydfil containing at present above 37,000
inhabitants, presents the most lamentable instance to the total
absence of all drainage.' The progress of another major
epidemic across the continent in 1847–48 was fast enough to
induce fear but slow enough to encourage preventive action.
The *Public Health Act of 1848* allowed for formation of *Local
Boards of Health* wherever ten per cent of the ratepayers
petitioned for one or wherever the death rate exceeded the
national average of 23 per 1,000 per year. Merthyr, quite the
worst town in Wales in this respect, had a rate of 34.7 per
thousand in the period 1847–53, only slightly behind the worst
areas of England.

Unbridled *laissez faire* seemed to threaten the stability and
survival of industrial society and *Benthamite* legislation to secure
greater happiness was the approved remedy. Prompted by
cholera, many areas in Wales established their *Local Boards of
Health*. In some towns they quickly provided the sewers,
drainage and clean water that was necessary and death rates
peaked and subsided. Cardiff's middle class scored a victory
against the *Bute estate* in this area and falling death rates were its
reward; 30 per 1,000 in the 1840s; 25.7 by the mid-6os and 22 per
thousand by the 1890s. In many other places with established
town governments and an assertive middle class who lived in
the midst of the insanitary conditions a similar story could be
told. In Neath, however, the body of small ratepayers created by
the break-up of the *Gnoll estate* proved to be an obstacle to
reform. In Merthyr, lacking in government and in middle-class
aggression, the power and parsimony of the great ironworking
concerns prevented any real progress for more than a decade.
Yet in the thirty years after 1850 the reformers won many
victories in the slow war of attrition against filth and disease. In
the 1870s two *Public Health Acts* established Urban and Rural
Sanitary districts to cover every locality. They varied greatly in
efficiency, competence and the degree of care shown, but the
framework for saving lives had been established. Children

A.10   under a year old continued to be the most vulnerable and new communities still had problems (A.10). In the 1870s the Rhondda Valleys were polluting their soil with 2,000–3,000 tons of excrement a year. Blaenau Ffestiniog, in a naturally healthy physical location, was an entirely man-made death trap with a mortality rate four times above that of a similar rural area in the 1870s.

The new towns seemed to be a moral threat too. In 1860 the Diocese of Llandaff established an institution for reclaiming prostitutes from their flourishing trade; it counted over 1,700 prostitutes in the towns of Cardiff, Merthyr, Swansea and Neath. The anonymity of the large towns, the migrant uprooted population, and the high incomes which bouts of industrial prosperity could give combined to create the circumstances, and the increasingly restricted employment opportunities for women supplied the passive bodies. Merthyr's rabbit-warren maze of low buildings near the river harboured prostitutes and their accomplices who robbed the customers, relying on embarrassment in order to escape pursuit and prosecution. This district rejoiced in the name of 'China', a 'no go' area for the authorities, symbolically ruled by a criminal Emperor and Empress. When the latter was transported in 1847 she flung a far-from-dainty boot across the court-room at her prosecutor as a token of her own and the whole district's defiance. Professional crime entrenched itself in 'China', but as the magistrates and the police began to come to terms with it around 1860, they were outflanked by the emergence of Cardiff's Butetown. China's 60 prostitutes and their pimps and accomplices were bad enough. Cardiff's 420 (sailors were much better customers than ironworkers) seemed to eat away at the recently laid

A.11   foundations of the town (A.11, A.12). Industrial towns had very
A.12   high rates of crime in the period, though in fact only a small
A.13   proportion of it was a full-time occupation (A.13). Much was a means of survival in an insecure and changing world; widows stealing coal and children stealing food when need and opportunity beckoned were more typical than the professionals.

The towns of the early industrial era are often regarded as frontier towns, places with few amenities, fewer traditions and a violent social life. Often they were, but we should be cautious of applying such a description to all towns at all phases of their development. The frontier of urbanization moved as fast as that of the American west. Periods of rapid growth and severe problems were succeeded by phases of slower growth when problems could be contained and coped with. Even Merthyr was showing signs of respectability and recognizable urban form by the mid-Victorian period and ultimately it would

A.14   develop the middle-aged spread of a corporation (A.14, A.15).

A.15   The frontier had moved on by then to Cardiff and the suburb of Cathays which sprung up around the Taff Vale Railway works seemed singularly lacking in amenities — roads, drains, a police station. Yet it quickly became the area of the town with the lowest turnover of population, a place where Co-operative stores and radical politics did better than in the rest of Cardiff

A.16   (A.16, A.17, A.18). It even acquired a police station. In the late
A.17   nineteenth century the Chief Constable of Cardiff thought that a
A.18   police station had a 'wonderfully civilizing effect on a certain
A.19   portion of the population' (A.19). Certainly the crime rates began to be checked though more widespread and stable prosperity probably had more impact than policing. The presence of the police on the streets (all counties and boroughs had to maintain forces from 1856 onwards) certainly changed the outward behaviour of many groups; vagrants, prostitutes, street-traders and noisy adolescents became more circumspect; publicans regulated their customers for the sake of their licences; brothels became less publicity-conscious and gamblers, prize fighters and blood sports enthusiasts needed to find places of seclusion well protected by look-outs to carry on their

A.20   activities (A.20). By the 1870s the streets seemed much safer for the middle classes with the new board schools pouring much oil on their troubled waters. Drink, which had been as vital a lubricant of the new industrial society as grease, became more manageable. Shorter working hours spread out consumption through the week and reduced the numbers of weekend trips to oblivion which the new society had induced. Penny readings, theatres and music halls came to provide less drastic means of escape and forgetting.

    Slowly the organs of local government became better able to cope. After 1858 most mining communities grew within a framework of local government and the lag in the provision of facilities was much shorter. A new community like Merthyr Vale which sprang up in the 1870s had effective sanitary and water supplies from the beginning. After 1875 houses had to be built to specifications laid down in local authority by-laws. The uniformity of the terraces increased, but so too did the size and salubriousness of the houses. By the 1880s it was surviving pockets of older housing which caused concern, not the new constructions. In the 1850s the opposite had been the case (A.9, A.10).

New towns revealed the passing of the frontier in their increasingly complex social divisions. In eighteenth-century towns social mixture within small areas had been the norm, with the rich tending to collect in the more prestigious central areas. The noxious fumes of industrialization drove the wealthy to the fringes, as the larger towns, at least, developed suburbs. The central areas became the preserve of shops and other businesses with working-class housing acting as a spacer. The more organized and coherent classes of Victorian society were leaving distinct impressions on the ground. Roads, railways, canals and docks marked social, not just physical, boundaries; people came to be born on the wrong side of the tracks. In Wales this process reached its peak in Cardiff's Butetown, a virtual island given over to the sailors and their temporary friends, where only resolute male business men would pass them on their way to dockside offices. The nearby centre of the town was divided off by a chasm of class and physical obstacles. New middle-class suburbs were much further away and protected the young and the female from the health and moral dangers of contamination. That which reached its peak in Cardiff was reproduced in all large towns, but not entirely absent in much smaller communities. In a deceptively simple quarry-town like Bethesda a similar process of social grading was under way. In 1851, 75 quarrymen lived in its main street, but twenty years later only 16 remained, most of the gaps having been filled by tradesmen, professionals and their businesses as a distinct commercial centre began to emerge. The common name 'Commercial Street' marks the same process in the south Wales valleys.

The greatest challenge to the frontier came from the people of the new industrial towns themselves. Commentators on the life of these communities often operated from such a long range that they failed to see the intricate social networks that emerged. The Welsh writer D.J. Williams disparaged '. . . the industrial parts of Glamorganshire where people begin to lose hold of each other and sink out of sight to the great rootless proletarian morass'. People left rural Wales in search of a better paid and more satisfying way of life, and came to the industrial towns not naked but clothed in the culture of their homelands. Village, family and county loyalties were recreated in Merthyr as elsewhere as people settled near relatives and friends in neighbourhoods which were much less unfriendly than they seemed to outsiders (A.21, A.22). In rural Wales they disciplined adulterers and wife-beaters with the ritual mockery of the *ceffyl pren* procession; in the Black Domain it was *blacklegs* who were the targets, but the methods were reassuringly similar. Chapels had begun to grow in rural Wales in the eighteenth century; transplanted to industrial Wales they flourished. In Merthyr Vale there were four chapels, with seats for 2,200 people, built within ten years of the sinking of the pit before the township was half built. This was a clear indication of shared values and social cohesion. Migrants also took their language with them; most industrial communities remained essentially Welsh-speaking in 1880, though all showed a tendency for bilingualism to develop.

Anglicization was still far off, except in the south Wales ports which drew increasing numbers of migrants from England. In the Rhondda it was Welsh-born people and usually Welsh speakers who migrated, and this could be even more emphatically stated for the Swansea valley or particularly the slate-quarrying communities which were the least cosmopolitan of Welsh industrial towns. In south Wales there was a mixing of cultures, and distinct ghettos in some cases, but Welsh was frequently still the language of pit and home and one which outsiders were obliged to learn if they valued social survival.

Not all community life was transplantation; new locations gave new opportunities, and new growth. Trade unions, *Friendly Societies* and political activity developed, as did the

A.21
A.22

competitive *eisteddfodic* culture flourishing in pubs at first, but moving into the domain of the chapel by the 1850s. Chapel, *eisteddfod*, *Friendly Society*, union and *Radicalism* nourished conceptions of self-improvement and seriousness. Not all were able, or wanted, to join this respectable world of the collier, quarryman and artisan — pubs as well as chapels were crowded though the two were not mutually exclusive — but it did exercise an influence over the life of the new towns. Uprooted this migrant society may have been, but it was not rootless or lonely. Surviving customs and beliefs were blended with the different demands and opportunities of the new order. Polish-Americans drew on two societies for their culture; so did *Cardis* in Merthyr.

By the 1880s a new civilization was apparent. Social observers thought it much less terrifying than they had in the 1830s; it was Welsh, respectably behaved and fundamentally in control of its health problems, even if pockets of anxiety remained. The very size of the towns made the key elements in Welsh life and their influence reach out far into the countryside. Young people were sucked out of Cardiganshire and mid-Wales at a rate which induced fears about their viability as societies. The urban printing presses spread their message into rural hinterlands, and rural industries collapsed one after another. Soon it would be the rural areas in which problems of public health and housing were most apparent for they lacked the will and the reformers to tackle the task in the way the towns had done. The spreading influence of the town is perhaps the ultimate indicator of the triumph of urbanization. In the eighteenth century the countryside had penetrated town walls with market gardens and other signs of agricultural pursuits. Paul Sandby's painting of eighteenth-century Cardiff shows pigs feeding in Crockherbtown. By 1901 Crockherbtown had expelled pigs in favour of huge shops and the even grander Park Hotel, and it was now called Queen Street in recognition of the Victorian prosperity which had transformed it. Cardiff was 'the Metropolis of Wales', dominating a huge area. The spread of urbanization bemused many people. Nostalgia for rural simplicity soothed the nerves and seemed to many the essence of Welshness. But deep down, Victorians knew that the real heart-beat of Wales was in the urban and increasingly democratic society which had emerged during the century.

Sources

A.1   *Borough of Bangor*
An obscure tradition appears still to linger there, that the city of Bangor was formerly incorporated; that it is a city, the seat of a most ancient bishoprick is alone sufficient to render such a tradition extremely probable. A person who long resided there stated that he recollected having formerly seen an old man, who was called 'the alderman' and the last alderman of Bangor; but he was always intoxicated and whether he was so called in jest on that account, or seriously from having filled a corporate office, was not known. Nor was any evidence of a less equivocal character communicated in support of the tradition . . . Bangor . . . together with Port Penrhyn, appears to promise a very rapid augmentation of population, wealth and commercial importance.

(British Parliamentary Papers, 1835, Vol.XXVI. *Reports from Commissioners on Municipal Corporations in England and Wales*, Vol.6.)

A.2   *Merthyr Tydfil*
Nothing can be more irregular and offensive to the eye, probably nothing more injurious to the health of the inhabitants, than the arrangement of the streets and houses. Indeed it is scarcely correct to say that there is in the place no place which can properly merit the name of a street. The houses were originally erected in the situation which best suited the convenience of the proprietor of the ground, without any regard to plan, or the situations of any similar buildings. As the increasing population called for new erections, the same method was successively followed, until the present collection of houses arose, spreading out over an immense extent of ground in every possible direction, communicating with each

other for the greater part by narrow lanes and avenues, which are generally choked with filth.

(Revd T. Rees, *A Topographical and Historical Description of South Wales*, 1813, pp.646–7.)

A.3 Long before you reach Merthyr, the blackened atmosphere points out the site; but when immediately upon it, you are obliged to inquire where it is, and the way to it ... After passing these (the *Plymouth Works*) you appear entering on an extended suburb of a large town; but the town itself is nowhere visible; it is without form or order; in short to get to your inn you can scarcely find your way along the main road; for to dignify it with the name of street, is more than it merits; yet here there is collected together a larger and more bustling population than any town in the principality can boast; its markets are large, well attended, and more than reasonable; its shopkeepers are numerous and thriving; and all that seems to be required to make the town one of the most respectable in the principality is, a little attention to order and cleanliness ...

(*The Cambrian Tourist or Post Chaise Companion through Wales* ...,
6th edition, London, 1828, pp.39–44.)

A.4 Merthyr Tydfil and Aberdare depend for their prosperity entirely upon the mineral wealth of the District in which they stand. The country supplies a rich Iron Ore, Coal close to it for smelting, and limestone for flux. The Population in both these places has grown up rapidly with the advance of the Iron Trade, and has been checked by its depression. The consequence is, that the Houses are, in a very great proportion, made up of Labourers' Cottages, or of small Ale-houses and beer shops, or of retail shops for supplying the wants of the population in which the higher, and middle orders form a very small ingredient, but which, for a labouring class is remarkably well paid, fed, lodged, and clothed.

The Population is of the most fluctuating kind; a slight improvement or depression in the Iron Trade increases or diminishes it by thousands. There are 24 furnaces in the Parish; the stoppage of one of these throws out of employment, not only a large number of workmen, but a great quantity of persons who supply the working population. The work in which labourers are employed is one which requires less experience than many other manufactures; so that a demand for labour is readily met by a supply; while, on the other hand, the labourers feel no great reluctance to transfer themselves to fresh employments.

(British Parliamentary Papers, 1832, Vol.XI, Part VIII. *Reports from Commissioners on the Proposed Division of Counties and Boundaries of Boroughs*, Vol.II, Part II, p.101.)

A.5   The season on the west coast is a good one . . . Criccieth, for instance, has been very full these last two weeks; Barmouth has a great gathering; and at Aberystwyth and the other watering places there is a general admission . . . that just now nothing need be complained of . . . Along the whole route of the Cambrian Railway are places which require only to be better known to be still more popular, for no district in the United Kingdom is so rich in natural scenery. The larger places on the northern coast have all the advantage which flows from their closer proximity to Liverpool and other great centres of population in Lancashire. Llandudno and Rhyl as the chief among them, have the greater number of visitors, the excellent service of steamers to the former being especially profitable, not only in bringing holiday-makers to the town, but also in providing them with first class trips while they are in residence . . . The dread of cholera on the Continent helped last year to turn holiday makers towards North Wales; and . . . it may be hoped that the appearance of cholera in Italy will induce a few more persons to come hitherward.

(*Caernarvon and Denbigh Herald*, 13 August 1886.)

A.6   Merthyr Tydfil with *Pen-y-Daran* and *Dowlais* may be regarded as chiefly a large cottage town, without any public care for the supply of water, drainage or cleansing, the open character and small height of its straggling buildings, and consequent exposure to sun and air, saving its population from still greater evils than those to which they are now exposed from the filth so abundant in it.

(British Parliamentary Papers, 1845, Vol.XVIII, p.151. Appendix to *Second Report of Commissioners of Inquiry into the State of Large Towns and Populous Districts.*)

A.7   Mr Landesborough (Principal Officer of Police):
. . . The chief nurseries are chiefly confined to the back streets, and consist of both streets and houses being in a filthy and unhealthy state, the yards being small and having privies in them, from which a disagreeable and unhealthy smell is emitted, and from which contagious diseases have frequently arisen. To several of the houses, especially those in Glan-yr-Afon, no privies are attached. The streets generally are rendered disagreeable from their want of being properly cleansed in the winter, and watered in summer. Water was very scarce in the summertime, until a few years ago a company erected works (which) affords a sufficient supply to all who apply for it. There is a general deficiency of drains in the town; those which are, being constructed on a principle which renders them of no use.
The houses in Kyffin-square and Glan-yr-Afon are dirty and badly ventilated. There is one tan-yard in Pendre High-street, one skinner's yard in Well-street and one in Dean-street, of which those who live in the neighbourhood complain.

(*Report to the General Board of Health on . . . the Borough of Bangor* by George Thomas Clark, London, 1849, p.8.)

A.8   Some of the back slums of the town, but especially the courts, were almost always nests of fever, and to add to this evil pigs in large numbers and in some instances cows were kept in such places, the animals being in many cases passed into the back yards through the houses . . . I was actuated by a strong and ardent desire to lower the high mortality rate of the town, and lead people into a higher and better life, . . . The owners of small houses regarded me as a sort of emissary of the Evil One . . . The suggestions I had long before made for obtaining a pure and efficient water supply and efficient drainage had been strongly opposed by members of the Corporation and others, but the cholera proved an efficient ally, and the order was made for both . . . During the raid I made on places unfit for human occupation I received some letters of warning, one of which was rather amusing. The writer, who I had no doubt was an owner of small houses, wrote strongly, urging me not to interfere with the dwellings of the poor, and advising me on no account to be out after dark, as there were many who suffered by my action who had determined to take my life . . . Daily evidence was afforded of the fact that poor uneducated people considered dirt and such odours as those of pigs to be exceedingly wholesome, and regarded sanitary action as a sad attack on their rights. Thank God the schoolmaster is abroad, and I trust cleanliness is one of the creeds he teaches . . . The folly and forgetfulness of the ignorant and uneducated are certainly most difficult to deal with; one hundred people had, by death from cholera, paid the penalty of living amid filthy surroundings, but it was nothing to the general decay and death due to dirt which has been going on for years . . . The town was drained, and an excellent supply of water obtained. Can any reasonable man doubt that had these and other precautions not been taken, many of those now alive, and many of those who lived for years after the cholera, would have paid the penalty of thus living in a filthy town, and would have joined the majority long before time? Yet many of these people were loud in the abuse of one whose aim was their good.

(*The Memories of Sir Llewelyn Turner*, ed. J.E. Vincent, London, 1903, pp.327–35. Turner was Mayor of Caernarfon during the cholera epidemic of 1866–67.)

A.9   Besides the parish churches and the Town Hall, there are few public buildings worthy of note; and the aspect of the town generally, with the exception of the principal streets, may be said to be on a par with many other country towns of a third or fourth class. It is very remarkable, and at the same time a fact upon which the improving and enterprising spirit of the age is not open to compliment, that the older part is the best, both as to the character and arrangements of the buildings, the houses in the newer part lying around the Docks and towards the East and South being of a very inferior description. [It is naturally very difficult to drain] . . . The consequence is what could only be looked for under such circumstances, floods, swamps, filth, miasma, ague and other disorders, in fearful abundance . . . The present drains throughout the town would be almost entirely useless in any future system of refuse-drainage. Perhaps the drains of two or three streets might be worked into such a system . . . Nothing can be worse than the house accommodation provided for the labouring classes and the poor in this town; and the overcrowding is fearful, beyond anything of the kind I have ever known of.

(Report to the General Board of Health on . . .the Sanitary Condition of the Inhabitants of the Town of Cardiff, by Thomas Webster Rammell, London, 1850, pp.11–32.)

A.10   Throughout the district the houses, as a rule are well and solidly built . . . In many places whole streets, or even, as at Llwynypia and Gilfachgoch, whole villages have been built by the proprietors of neighbouring collieries on a uniform plan. Elsewhere, also, in recent settlements, a certain uniformity obtains; but in the older villages, as Hafod and Stonehouse, the building is most irregular, and the convenience of systematic arrangement in great measure wholly disregarded. Here and there I saw hovels unfit for human habitation. The ground on which the floors are laid is seldom drained and little care is taken to keep the walls and foundations free from damp. Eaves-gutters, and main spouts are wanting in a large proportion of the cottages . . . rain pours with force . . . on to the ground or uncemented flags at the foot of the wall, and scoops out a hole in the earth or in the interstices of the stones and lies there in a pool, soaking into the foundations and making the dwellings damp and unwholesome. It must be remembered that the rainfall in this part of the country is excessive.

(Dr Airy's Report to the Local Government Board on the Sanitary State of the Pontypridd Registration District (Glamorganshire), 25 March 1876, pp.6–7.)

Newtown, Montgomeryshire, *c.* 1900. (*Source: National Library of Wales.*)

A.11   Then we proceeded to Pontystorehouse [a district of Merthyr] commonly called *China* and spent some hours conversing and reading with those given up to their own lusts and never enter the house of God at any time . . .

Ann Jenkins a China prostitute called upon me . . . she felt exceedingly under our preaching . . . that we were finding her sins out all along and that she made up her mind there and then to abandon her present mode of living at once . . . she is forty years of age, married and lived with her husband several years before he gave himself up to drink — not giving her any support and at times abused her shamefully. That she had one child and that she was supporting herself by washing about the houses — and falling into bad company she began to drink to excess and at last gave herself up to prostitution.

Furthermore she said that China is deserted by its visitors almost entirely . . . there are no men going there but *the vilest of the vile*. That some of the clerks of the town and well dressed men used to go there until we went there . . . the standard price is coming down from 1/- to 6*d.* and from 3/- per night to 1/6*d.*

(National Library of Wales MS 4943(B). *The Scripture Reader's Journal 1860.*)

A.12   Sir,

What a pity it is that our stipendiary and borough magistrates can not be compelled to take up their residence in Butetown for one year . . . Almost every street at the back of Bute Road has its low beer house or other licensed establishment, and as a rule, with two or three brothels right and left; and in the front of these houses may be seen drunken sailors of all nations and prostitutes dragging each other about in the most obscene and disgusting manner. In vain do the police resort to these cases, for though it is notorious that many of these drinking establishments are systematically kept open for the ingress and egress of these classes, yet a conviction is scarcely possible before the Cardiff magistrates.

A VOICE FROM BUTETOWN
(Letter in *The Cardiff Times*, 30 August 1861.)

A.13   *The Lawless Part of the Community*

The races this week attracted between 200 and 250 thieves of all grades to our town. Two or three watch robberies on the race-course and in the street have been reported, which with the rifling of Mr Whiffen's shop are the only depradations which have come to our knowledge. During the early part of the week the police watched the arrival of all the trains, and on nearly every occasion recognized groups of known thieves. Information was given once or twice a day to the proprietors of all jewelry shops and other 'likely' places, and to the vigilance of the police is undoubtedly due the fact that not a single burglary or serious robbery has been committed. Most of our unwelcome visitors left by the various trains . . . but . . . a number of suspicious characters are still hovering about the town.

(*The Cardiff Times*, 24 April 1869.)

A.14   The populous town (Merthyr) which, with astonishing rapidity, has sprung into existence was, until lately a shapeless, unsightly cluster of wretched dingy dwellings; but have in recent years undergone much improvement as well as extension. It now contains some regular, well-built streets, a court-house, a market-house, several elegant private residences, a large number of respectable shops, four churches, and not fewer than thirty-six dissenting chapels.

(*Black's Picturesque Guide to Wales*, 1881, p.307.)

A.15   . . . any one who wants to see a town in the making should visit Newport. I happened to arrive in it at a moment which the oldest and therefore most prejudiced inhabitant would not consider inopportune. Three great events had taken place, and Newport was full of revelry by day and night. First, the Newport Free Library had been opened and celebrated by what the local papers called 'a monster procession'. The building stands in Dock Street, and is a very tolerable structure of its kind. The rooms are large and well-stocked with books and prints. The second was the opening of a new wing of the Infirmary; and the third and last was the transformation of a small square into a 'park' . . . One hears of the growth of towns; but here you see the people clapping their hands, and shouting over development with the delight of a young mother who looks into her baby's mouth and finds new teeth in it.

(W. Clark Russell, *The North East Ports and Bristol Channel*, Newcastle, 2nd edition, 1883, p.86.)

A.16   Cathays, a suburban district situated about a mile to the north of the passenger station in Crockherbtown, and in the neighbourhood of which, within the last few years, a small town has sprung into existence. The situation is a pleasant one, having enough of agriculture about it to make the locality what it really is — suburban. Still it is sufficiently near the town to be of access whenever the residents may desire to visit it for business or pleasure.

(*The Cardiff Times*, 7 July 1860.)

A.17   *Cathays — Religious Worship*. The above is the name of a largely peopled locality which has been called into existence by the number of persons employed at the Taff Vale Railway Company's works. There is no place for religious worship specially set apart but the Wesleyans have had a room there for some time, and are desirous of building a chapel, which shall cost £150 or £160.

(*The Cardiff Times*, 14 December 1860.)

A.18   . . . the state of Cathays . . . is a reproach which has been hurled at the Board of Health for years past; . . . The alarming prevalence of fever there, I believe is unequalled in any other quarter of Cardiff; the dismal condition of the place for want of proper lighting, is of the gloomiest and most discreditable nature; its neglect by, or for want of, the police — especially on Sundays — is at all times alarming; and the narrow and dangerous activity of the road leading to it from the North road over the Taff Vale railway is a reflection on the Board of Health . . . the public should know that there are at the present moment scores of houses at the Cathays [*sic*] the neglect of whose drainage is well known to be the cause of a vast amount of prevailing sickness; and the sluggish and dilatory progress of the drainage works . . . is in itself a positive source of danger.

(Letter from 'Suburban', *The Cardiff Times*, 15 January 1870.)

A.19   Cathays a few years ago, consisted of three medium sized streets, with a few small streets branching therefrom, the whole population not numbering more than 1,000. Now there are several streets containing each over 100 houses and the total population is probably not far short of 15,000. The religious wants of the people of the district have been fairly provided for — the Church of England, the Congregationalists, Baptists, Primitive Methodists, Bible Christians, Free Church of England and Wesleyan having opened places of worship in Cathays of a more or less pretentious character. But what has been done for the civil government of the district? Very little indeed. If a row takes place and a policeman is wanted, it may be necessary to go to Roath Police Station before one can be found.

(*The Cardiff Times*, 6 December 1884.)

A.20   There are many people — and we confess we are among the number — who think that gas lamps are a good police force in themselves.

(*The Cardiff Times*, 29 August 1862.)

A.21   *Merthyr*
The workmen who are perpetually immigrating, live together very much in clans, e.g., the Pembrokeshire men in one quarter, the Carmarthenshire men in another and so on . . .

(British Parliamentary Papers, 1847, Vol.XXVII: *Report of the Commissioners into the State of Education in Wales*, p.307.)

A.22   (a) . . . point of importance urged in the evidence adduced from the quarry districts of *North Wales* is that the population of the little villages referred to is not migratory, but a settled, home-loving population, who build a large portion of the houses themselves for their own occupation. With them the question is one of sentiment. They build to provide a permanent *home*, not for investment, and they become attached to the homes which they build.

(*Digest of the Select Committee on Town Holdings*, Vol.II, p.150, c.1887.)

A.23　My father was an Englishman. He was born in a small village called Creaton, Northamptonshire . . . At the age of ten my father was hired by a cattle dealer who took him and several other boys to Wales . . . After about three years of this unsettled life, his mother having died during his absence, my father lost all desire to return home. He found work in the coal mines in the town of Neath, South Wales . . . When he was about seventeen he met my mother, (and) at first they were unable to converse, since she could not speak English and he could not speak Welsh.

My father continued to work as a coal miner and learned to speak, read, and write in the Welsh language (Celtic) . . . to all intents and purposes he became a Welshman and was accepted as such by the Welsh people.

My parents were married in 1872 in the town of Neath. My father was twenty and my mother was seventeen.

(Wyndham Mortimer, *Organise! My Life as a Union Man*, Boston 1971, pp.1–2.)

Debating the Evidence

The first essay in this volume deals with a fundamental transformation in Welsh society in the nineteenth century, one which underpins many of the developments which will be considered in later essays. The transformation was caused by the urbanization of Wales and although Neil Evans reminds us that the experiences of industrialization and urbanization were not invariably linked, they normally went together. We will see the effect of such changes in the case of movements such as the *Scotch Cattle* and *Chartism*. Some of the changes they wrought in the political and religious life of Wales will also be touched upon. Even the

Rebecca protest — essentially rural but touching the fringes of semi-industrialized eastern Carmarthenshire — was affected by urbanization. As Dr Howell points out, it was depression in industrial south Wales and a consequent slump in demand for agricultural produce, causing the collapse in agricultural prices, that acted as one of the pressures on the people of south-west Wales. Neil Evans makes use of newspapers and official reports. He also uses two examples of autobiography. Autobiography is a potentially very valuable source which, however, needs careful handling. It provides that expression of individual, direct experience which the historian so often craves, but it is highly subjective and reliant on memory. The typicality, representativeness and reliability of such material varies tremendously. Neil Evans also uses examples of what are sometimes called travelogues — contemporary guides or descriptions produced by travellers to or in Wales. These bear some resemblance to newspapers or the reports of social investigators. They rely on direct experience and, particularly where the traveller/author is possessed of a sharp eye, they can prove evocative and rewarding. Again, however, there is the danger of atypicality and superficiality.

Source A.1
What point is being made in this source? What type of source do you consider this and what questions might you ask in assessing its reliability?

Source A.2
What does the author of this mean by the phrase 'nothing can be more irregular and offensive to the eye'? Is there any indication in the document that the author is biased?

Source A.3
In what way does this source reinforce the evidence in A.2?

Source A.4
Bearing in mind the statements made here about the conditions of the working classes in Merthyr and Aberdare, what questions might you ask about the reliability of this source? What other evidence might enable you to check these statements?

Source A.5
Unintentionally, this document tells us something of links between Wales and England. What are we told, and why might the information be significant for social historians of Wales?

Source A.6
This is the fourth piece of evidence relating to the town of Merthyr. Why do you think there is so much evidence in Parliamentary Papers on the subject?

Source A.7
How does this piece of evidence support a point Neil Evans makes about the relationship between industrialization and urbanization?

Source A.8
In what way are the weaknesses of autobiography as a historical source demonstrated here?

Source A.9
What is meant here by the phrase 'the improving and enterprising spirit of the age is not open to compliment'? In respect of attitudes to the conditions of working people in towns, what additional information does this source provide compared with Source A.8?

Source A.10
Compare the evidence on working-class housing here with that in Sources A.2 and A.3.

Source A.11
As evidence for the experience of working people what strengths does this source appear to have compared to earlier ones in this section?

Source A.12
What reasons might there be for this letter being anonymously written? How does its anonymity affect its impact?

Source A.13
What aspects of working-class life in nineteenth-century Wales come to light in this source? What effects of urbanization might be seen here?

Swansea in the 1850s.

Source A.14
What evidence is there here of changes which have taken place in Merthyr Tydfil by the 1880s and of the strength of *Nonconformity* in Wales? What questions might you ask about the reliability of this source?

Source A.15
What do we learn from this document of the opportunities which urbanization offered people? What questions need to be asked in considering the reliability and possible weaknesses of this source?

Source A.16
In what way might information here be seen as contrasting with earlier material we have encountered on urbanization in the nineteenth century?

Source A.17
What evidence does this document furnish as to reasons for the growth of *Nonconformity* in nineteenth-century Wales?

Source A.18
Compare the evidence here to that in Source A.16. What point seems to emerge about urbanization?

Sources A.19 and A.20
Why does Neil Evans make such use of the *Cardiff Times*?
What questions might you need to consider about the newspaper in assessing the value of evidence taken from it?

Source A.21
What point is Neil Evans illustrating in this source? What other possible sources could be consulted to check the accuracy of this evidence?

Source A.23
How typical might the experiences described here be said to be of south Wales in the nineteenth century? What appear to you to be the possible strengths and weaknesses of this source?

Discussion

The nineteenth century produced two major and relatively new types of source which help the historian gain insight into the rapid changes, dislocations and social eruptions which beset Wales during this period. One of these, of course, is newspapers and in his use of a series of extracts drawn from the *Cardiff Times* on the development of Cathays in Cardiff (Sources A.16, A.17, A.18, A.19) Neil Evans shows how newspapers can provide excellent material charting the process of urbanization. Then we have the reports and enquiries of Government commissions and Parliamentary committees. The growth of towns like Merthyr Tydfil, and the problems associated with their rapid development, attracted official investigators, as well as travellers and newspaper reports (Sources A.2, A.3, A.4, A.6, A.14, A.22). Again, the kind of evidence produced can be richly evocative but, as with newspaper reporting, questions have to be asked as to how evidence was collected, by whom, and how typical it is. With both types of source what we are too often denied is direct testimony from the people who underwent the experience of industrialization and urbanization (Source A.11 is the nearest we have to this type of direct testimony).

Thomas Gee. (*Source: National Library of Wales.*)

Parliament and People in
Mid-Nineteenth-Century Wales

IEUAN GWYNEDD JONES

Most political observers, but more especially those who were sympathetic to the policies of the radical *Nonconformist* wing of the Liberal party, believed that the outstanding characteristic of Welsh politics in the middle decades of the nineteenth century was the political apathy of the bulk of the people. 'Nid yw y genedl fel cenedl yn teimlo nemawr o ddyddordeb mewn gwleidyddiaeth' (The real nation takes very little interest in politics) was the considered judgement of the author of an influential Welsh handbook on electoral affairs, *Llawlyfr Etholiadaeth Cymru* (Welsh Electoral Handbook) by Revd John Jones (Llangollen 1867) (B.1). The publisher *Thomas Gee* of Denbigh, owner of the enormously influential newspaper *Baner ac Amserau Cymru* (Banner and Times of Wales), agreed with him, as did many of the leading ministers of religion such as Dr Thomas Price, minister of Calfaria *Baptist* Chapel, Aberdare, who at various times edited newspapers circulating widely in the industrial towns and villages of south Wales. Above all, it was the view of leaders of political pressure groups and especially the leaders of the Society for the Liberation of the Church from State Patronage and Control — the Liberation Society, as it was known. It was not a view subscribed to by all politicians, and many Liberals would have agreed with the *Tories* that this alleged political apathy was preferable to the fearful disturbances which had accompanied the emergence of radical politics in the late 1820s and 1830s.

The evidence for this apathy was mainly of two kinds. First, there was the difficulty experienced by local politicians and the leaders of political societies from outside Wales in persuading

B.1

Henry Richard. (*Source: BBC Hulton Picture Library.*)

men to take an active interest in local and national affairs, and to organize for the purpose of agitation by supporting the numerous political pressure groups active at that time. Both the *National Reform Union*, a largely middle-class society founded in

B.2   1864 to campaign for household *suffrage* (B.2), and the *Reform League*, a working-class organization founded in 1866 to

B.3   campaign for manhood *suffrage* and the ballot (B.3), found it difficult to establish strong and permanent branches in Wales. Men flocked to listen to lectures but were reluctant to give their financial and moral support. The author of *Llawlyfr Etholiadaeth Cymru*, himself a Vice-President of the *Reform League*, was of the opinion that if the people of England had shown as little interest in politics as the Welsh people the cause of Liberalism would not have advanced very far, and he suggested that the political backwardness of Wales may even have been a positive hindrance to the advance of Liberalism

B.1   (B.1). This was certainly the view of the most successful of the political societies working in Wales — the Liberation Society. This organization, which had been founded in 1844 and had had

B.4a   a presence in Wales ever since, and which since 1862 (B.4a) had been concentrating much of its very considerable resources in Wales, professed itself deeply disappointed with the kind of response it was getting and the practical results of its efforts

B.4b   (B.4b).

    Nor was this something new. *Henry Richard*, secretary of the *Peace Society*, a leading Liberationist and exponent of *Nonconformist* politics, was convinced that this was the normal condition of the Welsh people and was the product of their intensively exclusive religious culture and a consequence of the

B.5   lack of an indigenous political press (B.5). Twenty years earlier, the young Walter Griffith, stationed in Wales as a lecturer for the *Anti-Corn Law League*, made exactly the same points: the Welsh people were ignorant of politics and difficult to agitate. In his perambulations throughout the length and breadth of the Principality he had encountered an active response among the working classes only in those towns and villages where *Chartism* was strong — in those cases, a very active, well-informed and

B.6   intelligent opposition to the views he was propagating (B.6). *Chartism* and the protest movements of the previous half century or so were not so much ignored by these new politicians of the 1860s as explained away. *Chartism*, they proclaimed, was not an indigenous movement: like trade *unionism* it had been brought into Wales by disaffected Englishmen and had been

B.7   confined to the south eastern counties (B.7). The Rebecca Riots constituted an aberration from the normally peaceful state of affairs in the countryside and the movement, if it really was a

B.8   movement, was in no way political (B.8). In any event these rural risings had long since ceased, and *Chartism* survived only in a few places, lacking any organization, confined to middle-aged and middle-class men happy in their support of middle-class liberal Nonconformism. As Morgan Williams of Merthyr Tydfil, who had succeeded John Frost as the leader of Welsh *Chartism*, remarked in 1866, 'the working men did not have the political feelings of thirty years ago'. He and his fellow *Chartists* had long since abandoned their revolutionary principles and had come to embrace instead a more pragmatic, gradualist, reformist and deeply constitutional philosophy of political change.

Secondly, and more specifically, the evidence for this apathy was inferred from the contradiction between the religious life of the people of Wales and their representation in parliament. Wales was notorious for the pronounced *Nonconformist* character of its religion. *Henry Richard* devoted the third chapter of his book on the social and political condition of Wales to an analysis of the comparative strength of the Church and *Nonconformity* in order to show that the huge disproportions revealed in the *Religious Census of 1851* had, if anything, widened in the interval, and it was generally accepted that about three-quarters of the Welsh people were *Nonconformists*, from which it followed that 'the Church of England is not the Church of Wales'. *Henry Richard* thought of this immense social change as having happened in his lifetime (he was born in 1812), and the statistics do show that the relative strengths of the *established Church* and *Nonconformity* in 1851 was almost the complete

B.9   reversal of what it had been in 1801 (B.9).

Nor was there any mistaking the predominant strength of the older Dissenting denominations within *Nonconformity*. The *Independents*, the *Baptists* and the *Unitarians* — the *Quakers*

scarcely had a presence in Wales in the nineteenth century —
had all originated in the revolutionary times of the seventeenth
century, and all had behind them traditions of radical but
peaceful and constitutional protest and agitation in defence of
their legal rights and for religious equality with the *established
Church*. They had been accustomed, on and off, to acting
politically in the past: in 1828 they had succeeded in persuading
parliament to repeal the hated *Test and Corporation Acts* — that
body of legislation dating from 1661 which, though it had little
practical effect at the time, they regarded as a badge and symbol
of their inferior status as citizens. Some of the remaining
disabilities had been removed in 1836 with a new system of civil
registration of births, marriages and deaths, and the registration
of chapels as places in which marriages might take place. But
other grievances remained; notably the payment of *Church Rates*
for the upkeep of the parish church and of *tithes* for the
maintenance of incumbents; the fact that burials in parish
churchyards could be conducted only by clergymen of the
Church of England; and the exclusion of Dissenters from the
universities. These were grievances which could be redressed
only in Parliament because they all required the repeal of
statutes which asserted the supremacy of the *established Church*.
Not all *Nonconformists* felt all of them to be grievances. The
Methodist denominations, both the *Wesleyan Methodists* and the
Welsh Calvinistic Methodists, for example, frowned upon almost
any kind of formal political commitment and activity by the
individual congregations and denominational organizations.
But when, from about the middle of the century, fears grew that
the *established Church* was drifting in the direction of Rome, that
Anglo-Catholicism was corrupting the Protestantism which the
Church existed to defend, the *Methodists* became more ready to
co-operate in the political campaigns of Dissent. It is this which
explains the great upsurge in political feeling in the great
election of 1859 in Merioneth — an election which heralded the
coming of a new kind of politics.

But these social facts, the essential, defining social
characteristics of the Welsh people, were in no way reflected in
the representation of the people in Parliament. All the seventeen
county members were wealthy landowners and all resident as

proprietors in the counties they represented, and most of them belonged to families which had dominated the respective seats for many generations. Precisely these same upper-class landed families monopolized, or nearly so, the fifteen borough seats and hence the sixty representative towns or contributory boroughs. There were exceptions to this rule especially in constituencies such as those in Glamorgan and Monmouthshire, where powerful and rich ironmasters and coalowners were prepared to contest elections. But even these aggressive industrialists were also landowners on a large scale, and like all other great industrialists in Wales coming more and more to resemble, and in the end to be identified with, the great landowners. The system of representation was eloquent testimony to two related facts: first to the monolithic control of political life at that level by a small group of aristocratic dynastic and gentry families, and second, to the convergence in practical policies as in style and manner of life of the two major sources of wealth, agriculture and industry.

As important was the fact that all were Churchmen. It is true that a few were good Liberals whose votes could be relied upon by the *Nonconformists*, and at least one, the industrialist Lewis Llewelyn Dillwyn (elected for Swansea in 1855) though an Anglican was a leading Liberationist both in and out of Parliament. But none was identified religiously with the majority of the people either of the country as a whole or at constituency level. Radical newspapers, such as *Baner ac Amserau Cymru* and *The Liberator* (the organ of the Liberation Society), regularly published analyses of the votes of the Welsh members on issues of religious and civil equality with a view to publicizing the scandalous indifference of the members to the interests and feelings of their constituents (B.10).

B.10

This was why franchise reform became the main objective of *Nonconformist* politicians. The most radical among them advocated manhood *suffrage*, as had the *Chartists* before them; all wished to abolish the age-old property qualifications for the vote which the 1832 Reform Act had retained, and all wished to abolish other restrictions on the possession of the franchise, such as payment of rates and receipt of *Poor Law Assistance*, by which so many working men were disqualified and which made it possible for party managers to manipulate the votes of the working classes. It was the combination of these factors which kept the electorate small and which, in fact, ensured that the rise in the number of votes should not be commensurate with the rise in population. In the middle decades of the century population grew by 24 per cent, but the number of voters by only about 10 per cent (B.11). The same was true of the working class vote in the boroughs. In 1832 the vote had been given to £10 householders, and these were mainly the professional men, tradesmen and shopkeepers, artisans, and the top ranks of the working classes. The bulk of the working men who possessed the vote in 1832 would appear to have qualified as freemen or ancient rights voters for whom the possession of property would not necessarily have been a qualification. These were abolished by the Reform Act and as their possessors died out so the ranks of working class voters diminished (B.12). In Merthyr Tydfil, which had been enfranchised by the 1832 Reform Act and where there were therefore no freemen voters, and where the vast bulk of the population lived in rented accommodation, the number of voters was kept small by the rating requirements of the Act. These statutory conditions ensured that the voters were overwhelmingly middle class and that only a minute proportion of the working class should be enfranchised. The relative decline in the number of voters and the stringent conditions imposed by the law and exploited by party agents and managers was not an encouragement to participatory politics.

In the counties the problem of the franchise was somewhat different. The right to vote had been given, as was the case before the Reform Act, to men who owned freeholds of various kinds worth 40 shillings per annum or more and to certain kinds of leaseholders, and thus had enfranchised landowners, clergymen, farmers and substantial tenants. But it had also given the vote to small tenant farmers paying rents of £50 per annum or more for their farms and whose tenancies had to be renewed every year. These were the so-called tenants-at-will, small farmers who had no leases to protect them in the occupancy of their farms and who were therefore economically dependent upon their landlords for their livelihoods. This was a factor of

B.11

B.12

major importance in the shaping of Welsh political life. Wales was a land of huge landed estates and of great numbers of small tenant farmers. On average more than a quarter (27.6 per cent) of the total of county voters were tenants-at-will. In most of the north Wales counties the proportion was about a third of the total registered voters: in Merioneth more than a half were tenants-at-will (B.13). This was a major factor in Welsh politics because it ensured that, in the last resort, the great estates voted as a bloc. At best there would be a tacit understanding between tenants and landlords, and in a deferential system tenants would normally vote with their lords. But at worst there was the ever-present threat of eviction or of positive rent-rises — 'screwing', or the exercise of undue influence — to ensure that they did so. Usually tenants did as they were told but they could not necessarily be relied upon to do so. The classic case of tenant farmers, large and small, defying their landlords and refusing to vote for the *Tory* candidate occurred in Bala in the 1859 Merioneth election. Several tenants of the Glanllyn estate of Sir Watkin Williams Wynn and the Rhiwlas estate of R.W. Price were evicted in consequence (B.14). If nothing else, this demonstrated that there were limitations to the traditional electoral behaviour of dependent tenants, and that for many common people principle was more important than profit and religion than livelihood. In fact, the deferential structure of farming communities on the great Welsh estates ensured that, as a general rule, the landed proprietors could determine the party character of county representation.

Deference operated in the boroughs as well, especially in the small rural towns which were closely integrated into their agricultural hinterlands. It was not such a powerful social force in industrial boroughs — though it was often the objective of industrialists to replicate the political morality of the agri-cultural estates: and the exertion of influence over the voting intentions of borough voters generally took the form of bribery, or treating, or open or concealed threats on the part of employers. Pressure of this kind by ironmasters on their dependent workers, and the assumption that the machinery of local government was there to be manipulated for the benefit of the masters, was a fact of life in local government elections in

B.13

B.14

B.15   industrial towns, and deeply resented as such (B.15). The Rhondda coalowner Walter Coffin owed his unexpected return for the Cardiff boroughs in 1852 partly to the influence which the ironmasters of *Dowlais* and *Cyfarthfa* could exert over their
B.16   tenants and workmen in Cardiff (B.16). Merthyr Tydfil was not technically a *pocket borough* but it was inconceivable that anyone but the agreed nominee of the ironmasters could ever win the seat. As in the counties, the system of open voting in relatively small, face-to-face communities ensured that the wealthy and the powerful would always be able to influence the outcome of parliamentary elections. The Ballot, or secret voting, was demanded by radicals as the best means of putting an end to influence of this kind.

    In both borough and county constituencies the costs of elections were a fundamental hindrance to the democratic process. Only men with substantial private means, or the backing of aristocratic patrons (in which case their independence might be compromised) could bear the heavy expenses that were involved, or maintain themselves as members of parliament when elected. In pre-reform days election expenses could be astoundingly large. The *Whig* candidate William Paxton of Middleton Hall is said to have spent nearly £16,000 contesting the Carmarthenshire county seat in the election of 1802. But this was the 'Austerlitz of Welsh electioneering': there was nothing comparable in later elections, though very considerable sums
B.17a   were expended (B.17a). High election expenses had the effect of reducing the number of contested elections by encouraging local electoral pacts or agreements between parties, restricted the choice of electors as to the sort of man they wanted, and made it virtually impossible for members of the working class to stand for parliament. *Chartists* put up their own candidates in Merthyr Tydfil and in Monmouth in 1841, but in the nature of things these were gestures only, defiant demonstrations by the unenfranchised and the disenfranchised, and opportunities too good to be missed to express their solidarity, rare episodes in
B.17b   their political education (B.17b).

    To what extent the activities of the reformers helped to bring about the Reform Act of 1867 is a matter for debate, but it is certain that the highly organized and efficient agitation of the

Henry Austin Bruce. (*Source: BBC Hulton Picture Library.*)

Liberation Society in Wales rekindled the political traditions of Dissent and politicized the chapels. But the shape and details of the Act were determined by the exigencies of party conflict within the House of Commons. Even so, the coming of household *suffrage* in the boroughs and a slight widening of the franchise in the counties profoundly changed the pattern of politics. The number of voters more than doubled (B.18a), and in the subsequent election of 1868 'the ice of *Toryism* was broken' and with it the apathy and indifference upon which it had been based. In Merthyr Tydfil the huge increase in the electorate enabled the working classes, especially the colliers, to assert themselves independently of the official Liberal leadership and to bring to the forefront of the campaign issues like industrial relations and *unionism* (B.18b). Indeed, the Merthyr election was as much a victory for working class *Radicalism* as for the *Nonconformist Radicalism* of *Henry Richard*. Among the Liberal majority were three Welsh *Nonconformists*. More important even than that was the inevitability of further change in the direction of a fuller degree of democracy. The Ballot Act was passed in 1872 which, in due course, gave the voters the reassurance of free and equal voting which they had long sought (B.19). Other measures followed, culminating in the *Reform and Redistribution Acts of 1884/5* which brought in yet another of the old *Chartist* demands, equal electoral districts. But it was still manhood *suffrage*: few Welshmen demanded equal rights for women.

B.18a

B.18b

B.19

Sources

B.1   *Anfanteision y Cymry gyflawni eu dyledswydd.* Yn gyntaf, nid yw y genedl fel cenedl yn teimlo nemawr o ddyddordeb mewn gwleidyddiaeth. Dyma ydyw y ffaith, nas gellir ei gwadu . . . Gallwn fod yn sicr pe y buasai y genedl Seis'nig wedi teimlo cyn lleied o ddyddordeb mewn gwleidyddiaeth a'r Cymry, y buasai yr achos mawr rhyddfrydig yn llawer nes yn ol nag ydyw yn bresennol. Nid yw y cymhorth a roddodd Cymru iddo ond y peth nesaf i ddim: ac mewn rhai amgylchiadau yr oedd yn rhwystr i gerbyd rhyddid i fyned rhagddo yn fuddygoliaethus. Mor tawel heb ei aflonyddu gan yr un don . . . yw cyflwr gwleidyddol Cymru wedi bod am dair canrif a rhagor. Pan unwyd Cymru a Lloegr, dan deyrnasiad Henry VIII, ac yr estynwyd gweinyddiad y deddfau Seis'nig iddi, ac y caniatawyd iddi ran yn rhagorfreintiau y deyrnas, darfyddodd terfysg o'i mewn, ac eisteddodd y genedl yn dawel wrth draed eu gorchfygwyr; ac oddiar hyny hyd yn awr, y mae y genedl wedi ymollwng i gyflwr o glaerineb a difaterwch gwleidyddol . . . Y mae anwybodaeth yn bodoli yn mhlith mwyafrif y werin ar bynciau gwladol, a theimlad yn cael ei feithrin oddiar hyn nad oes a fyno hwy yn bersonnol a hyn . . . Y teimlad mewn gwirionedd yw, na pherthyn gwleidyddiaeth iddynt hwy, ond i ereill: a gadawant ef i ofal y cyfryw rai. Credwn yn ddiysgog mai dyma deimlad mwyafrif y genedl Gymreig, er bod yma eithriadau gogoneddus.

(Llawlyfr Etholiadaeth Cymru, gan y Parch J. Jones, Llangollen 1867, tt.115–16.)

(The disadvantages of the Welsh in fulfilling their duty. First, the nation as a nation has felt [lit. feels] hardly any interest in politics. This is the fact that cannot be denied . . . We can be certain that if the English nation had felt [lit. feels] as little interest in politics as the Welsh, the great liberal cause would have been much more behind than it is at present. The support that Wales has given to it is next to nothing: and in some instances it was an obstruction to the chariot (carriage) of freedom to go ahead victoriously. A calm sea untroubled by a single wave . . . that has been the state of the politics of Wales for more than three centuries. When Wales and England were united in (under) the reign of Henry VIII, and the English laws were applied to her, and she was given a share of the privileges of the kingdom, internal turmoil ceased, and the nation sat quietly at the feet of the victor; and from that day to this, the nation has let herself go into a lukewarm state and political indifference . . . Ignorance about national issues exists among the majority of the people, and out of this is nurtured a feeling that they are not involved personally . . . In fact the feeling is

that politics does not belong to them but to others: and they leave it to the care of these others. We believe emphatically that this is the feeling of the majority of the Welsh nation, although there are glorious exceptions.)

(*Election Handbook of Wales* by the Revd J. Jones. Translated by D.A.T. Thomas.)

B.2   *The National Reform Union*: Statement
That while the statements made in this Conference [in May 1862] show the deep conviction of the people in favour of Manhood *Suffrage*, in which conviction a large proportion of the delegates fully sympathized, the Conference considers that the union of all classes of real Reformers is essential to the attainment of any real improvements of the representation, and with this view it submits to the country the following programme as a basis for action: Such an extension of the franchise as will confer the *suffrage* upon every male person, householder or lodger, rated or liable to be rated for the relief of the poor, together with a more equable distribution of seats, vote by ballot, and a limitation of the duration of Parliament to three years.

(The National Reform Conference, May 15 and 16, 1865. Quoted in S. Maccoby, *The English Radical Tradition 1763–1914*, 2nd ed., 1966, pp.162–4.)

B.3   The *National Reform League*: Manhood *Suffrage* and the Ballot
We shall again soon be called to agitate for the following measures:

I   The abolition of restrictions relative to the mode of paying rates upon which the franchise is based.
II   The equalization of the county and borough franchises.
III   A new and improved distribution of seats.
IV   The Ballot, to protect the voter . . .
V   If not for annual, at least for Triennial Parliaments . . .

(The League's Midland Department *Second Annual Report from July 1866 to July 1867*. Quoted in Maccoby, op.cit., pp.164–65.)

B.4a   Looking at the great preponderance of *Nonconformity* in Wales, and to the fact that it is at present scarcely represented in Parliament, we think it important that a special and decided Electoral effort should be made in that part of the Kingdom.

(Minute 120b, 27 September 1861. Minute Book of the Executive Committee of the Liberation Society, Greater London County Record Office, MS A/Lib/2, Minute 1207.)

B.4b   Resolution 2 — 'That this Conference views with the utmost dissatisfaction the mode in which Wales is represented in the Imperial Parliament — a nation of *Nonconformists* being without a single *Nonconformist* representative, and many of the constituencies being represented by members who are altogether wanting in sympathy with, if not actually opposed to, the religious and political convictions of an overwhelming majority of the Welsh people. That it believes that the time has come when a united, persistent, and courageous effort should be made to put an end to so glaring an anomaly, and therefore calls upon the Welsh Voluntaries to prepare themselves for such electoral movements as will be best adapted to secure the object.'

(*Welsh Nonconformity and the Welsh Representation. Papers and Speeches read and delivered at the conferences held in September and October 1866.* Liberation Society, n.d., p.ix.)

B.5   And, in the first place, it must be confessed, that it is only within a comparatively late period that the Welsh people have begun to take an intelligent and earnest interest in politics. Not but that the Principality before that was sometimes as violently agitated as other parts of the country by electioneering excitements: but usually the conflict turned much more upon persons than principles. Certain great families, who by tradition or accident, rather than from conviction, had come to espouse one side or the other in politics, held it a matter of hereditary honour to contest the representation with each other, far less as a means of giving effect to any particular views of State policy, than of asserting and maintaining their own family consequence against rival claimants in a county or neighbourhood. In times

preceding the religious revival of the last century the bulk of the
people were content to leave the question of political principle,
if indeed any such were involved, in the hands of these local
magnates, enlisting under the banners they unfurled with
unquestioning faith and devotion. Whatever of enthusiasm,
therefore, they felt in electioneering struggles was less that
of citizens contending for their rights than of clansmen
vehemently battling for their respective chieftains . . .

. . . there came upon Wales a season of great political apathy.
It was a period of transition. The time for the politics of blind
partisanship was gone. The time for the politics of intelligent
conviction had not yet come. One formidable obstacle in the
way of this was the difference of language, which cut the people
off from the political literature of England. At first, their own
periodical literature, being, like almost everything else that was
good among them, the offspring of the religious revival, took
its character from the cause from whence it had arisen. It was
almost exclusively religious. I remember when I was a boy that
all the politics of the magazine received in my father's house
were compressed into about half a page of the most insipid
summary at the end.

(Henry Richard, *Letters on the Social and Political Condition of the
Principality of Wales*, 1st ed., 1866, pp.79–80 and 83.)

B.6   The people of Wales, though they are in some degree informed,
yet they never bore a *political* character. They read much, but it
is chiefly on religious subjects. There are certainly great
numbers of people that do read newspapers, and know a little
about the affairs of the nation, but in general terms these men
are landlords and *aristocratic* tradesmen, and will not come to
hear anything that is contrary to their opinion. My audiences are
generally made up of working people, who do not understand
the English language . . . As for forming Associations, they are
wholly inexperienced; they have no taste for such a thing. They
are ready to assist the cause with their prayers, with their names
to petitions, and with their mites towards a public collection,
but they say they have no time, nor the power of forming
Associations. There is a numerous body of religious men who

possess a very great influence with the working classes. This body has been *generally* against any political movement; their chief men denounce from the pulpit those who are the means of getting up a petition to parliament, be it on what subject it may. There was never any question bearing on politics discussed throughout the Principality before the *corn law* question, which has excited great interest in many places.

(*Anti-Corn Law* Circular, no.44, 8 October 1840, quoting a letter from Walter Griffith. Quoted in full in Ieuan Gwynedd Jones, 'The Anti-Corn Law Letters of Walter Griffith', *Bulletin of the Board of Celtic Studies*, XXVIII, Part I (November 1978), pp.118–19.)

B.7   One very prominent fault of our working men is their readiness to allow themselves to be made the dupes of cunning and designing men. Several instances of this have occurred in the counties of Monmouth and Glamorgan within the last thirty-five years. About the year 1833, a cunning Welshman named Twist, who pretended to be a most sincere friend of the working classes, visited Merthyr and other places on the Hills, where he induced thousands of the people to form themselves into a kind of Workingmen's Union for the professed purposes of defending their rights against the tyranny of the masters, and raise the price of labour by refusing to instruct any workmen from the agricultural districts in mining operations. The designing originator of the Union gained his object by securing to himself large sums of money from his dupes, but his plausible scheme led to nothing better than the horrid nocturnal doings of the *Scotch Cattle*, and a series of ruinous strikes which brought hundreds of families to the brink of starvation. The *Chartist* movement of the year 1839 originated in a similar manner. A number of mob orators came down from England, who, by their thundering declamation against the oppression and injustice of the aristocracy, and fair promises of a perfect earthly paradise to the working classes as soon as the points of the charter would become the law of the land, soon gathered around their standard hundreds of confident expectants of the best things on earth. But, in the course of a few months all their

high expectations ended in a disgraceful riot, poverty, imprisonment, and death.

(Thomas Rees, 'The Working Classes of Wales', in *Miscellaneous Papers on Subjects Relating to Wales*, 1867, p. 19.)

B.8 Thus far, at any rate, it is true that from that time to this (i.e from the *Act of Union*) the Welsh people have been unswervingly loyal to the English government . . . For the last hundred and fifty years there is probably no part of the United Kingdom that has given the authorities so little trouble or anxiety. Anything like sedition, tumult, or riot is very rare in the Principality. There have been only two considerable exceptions to this rule, and these are more apparent than real. The first was the *Chartist* outbreak in Newport in 1839. But this was almost entirely of English inspiration, and spread over one corner of Wales, that occupied by the mixed and half-Anglicized population of Monmouthshire and the other adjacent coal and iron districts. The great bulk of the Welsh people had no share whatever in the movement, but looked upon it with undisguised repugnance and horror. The Rebecca disturbances of 1843 undoubtedly differed widely in this respect, that they broke out in the very heart of the purely Welsh population. But the character of these also has, I believe, been greatly misunderstood in England. They had no political significance whatsoever, and implied no disaffection to the government. They were merely uprisings, to which the men were driven, or imagined themselves driven, by the pressure of a grievance that had become intolerable, and against which they had long in vain protested and appealed . . . No doubt, as the thing went on, there were symptoms that a few evil-minded persons were disposed to turn the agitation to account for other and more serious purposes.

(Henry Richard, *Letters*, op.cit., pp. 72–3.)

B.9 PROPORTIONAL STRENGTH OF THE MAIN DENOMINATIONS IN
SOUTH WALES AND NORTH WALES

DENOM	% PLACES		% SITTINGS		% ATTEND	
	Nth	Sth	Nth	Sth	Nth	Sth
Church	22.55	33.01	31.27	29.72	17.41	18.76
Independents	16.91	19.69	14.57	23.87	15.92	28.45
Baptists	8.85	15.94	6.45	17.43	8.52	21.26
Wesleyan	20.07	11.21	15.52	8.26	22.06	7.40
Calv. Method.	29.61	16.21	30.68	17.89	39.65	21.09

(Religious Census of 1851)

Indexes for whole of Wales

Popn.   1,005,721
Accom.   778,202 = 77.37   N Wales 83.14   S Wales 73.37
Attend.   852,024 = 84.71   N Wales 86.62   S Wales 83.39

B.10 THE VOTES OF WELSH MEMBERS OF PARLIAMENT ON
ECCLESIASTICAL QUESTIONS — SUMMARY OF VOTES

	For.	Against.	Liberal. absent.	Conser. absent.
Qualification for Offices Bill	3 votes	0	15	14
Church-rates Bill	17 votes	4	1	10
Parliamentary Oath Bill	9 votes	9	9	5
Oxford Tests Bill, 2nd Reading	11 votes	3	7	11
Fellow of College Bill	10 votes	7	8	7
Oxford Tests Bill, Committee	14 votes	9	4	5

(*Welsh Nonconformity and the Welsh Representation. Paper and Speeches read and delivered at the conferences held September and October 1866*, Liberation Society, n.d., p.12)

B.11   TABLE 1. THE COUNTY FRANCHISE

COUNTY	Registered Voters as Percentage of Population		
	in 1832	in 1866	in 1868
Anglesey	3.9	5.7	9.4
Caernarfon	3.5	3.0	6.2
Denbigh	3.5	6.4	9.0
Flint	5.0	5.9	7.9
Montgomery	5.7	5.8	9.8
Merioneth	2.2	3.9	6.8
North Wales	4.5	5.3	8.1
Monmouth	5.2	3.7	5.1
Glamorgan	6.7	4.7	7.0
Carmarthen	6.1	5.4	9.0
Pembroke	6.0	5.9	6.3
Cardigan	3.2	5.6	8.2
Brecon	5.5	4.5	4.5
Radnor	10.5	8.7	12.0
South Wales	5.5	4.6	6.8
Welsh Counties	5.2	5.1	7.3

TABLE 2. THE BOROUGH FRANCHISE

BOROUGH	Registered Voters as Percentage of Population		
	in 1832	in 1866	in 1868
Beaumaris	3.1	4.2	14.2
Caernarfon	5.2	4.7	12.2
Denbigh	7.2	5.0	13.8
Flint	8.4	3.7	14.3
Montgomery	4.2	5.6	13.7
North Wales	5.8	4.7	13.5
Monmouth	8.6	6.5	9.7
Cardiff	8.3	4.5	9.0
Merthyr Tydfil	1.8	1.4	15.0
Swansea	4.2	3.1	9.3
Carmarthen	5.1	3.6	12.4
Pembroke	10.8	5.9	10.2
Haverfordwest	8.6	8.2	16.1
Cardigan	10.3	6.0	10.8
Brecon	4.6	5.4	12.8
Radnor	8.3	6.0	11.8
South Wales	6.4	3.8	11.4
Welsh Boroughs	6.0	4.0	11.9

(Based on Electoral Returns published in Parliamentary Papers)

B.12 NUMBER OF WORKING CLASS ELECTORS IN WELSH BOROUGHS IN 1866

BOROUGH	REGISTERED ELECTORS				WORKING CLASS ELECTORS				
	£10	Free	Other	Total	£10	Free	Other	Total	%
Beaumaris	561	2		563	180			180	33.1
Brecknock	293	12		281	82			82	27.9
Cardiff	1889	234		2123	662	122		784	36.5
Cardigan	637	55		692	83	5		88	12.7
Carmarthen	775	41		816	152			152	18.6
Caernarfon	1027		66	1093	177		31	208	19.0
Denbigh	805	129		934	86	76		162	16.5
Flint	601		99	700	161		51	212	28.1
Haverfordwest	406	191	215	812	116	113	82	311	38.3
Merthyr	1387			1387	126			126	9.1
Montgomery	954	61		1015	171	40		211	20.7
Pembroke	1102	377		1479	515	284		799	54.0
Radnor	420	24		444	51	1		52	11.7
Swansea	1695	312		2007	366	96		462	27.2
	12552	1426	380	14358	2928	737	164	3829	26.6
Monmouth	2125	21		21416	825	10		835	38.8
Wales	14677	1447	380	35774	3753	747	164	4664	38.5

Note what is meant by 'working class' in the above table.

'The Board do not intend that the Return should be exclusively confined to journeymen who are employed for wages, but that it should include men who work daily at their handicraft trade without a master, and even sometimes employ a journeyman or apprentice, provided that they derive their chief support from their own labour, and not from the labour of others, or the profits arising from capital or the supply of materials.'

(From a letter to Overseers from the Poor Law Board, 2 January 1866.)

Note also that the total of registered working class electors includes 127 electors who were registered in respect of more than one qualification. These were distributed as follows: Cardiff — 9; Cardigan — 1; Denbigh — 7; Flint — 6; Haverfordwest — 66; Montgomery — 14; Pembroke — 23; Swansea — 1.

(P.P. 1866 LVII (3626) and (296).)

B.13 Tenants-at-will as proportion of total number of voters.

	1835	**1865**
Anglesey	32.2	24.4
Brecon	27.0	26.3
Cardigan	35.0	23.3
Carmarthen	23.0	27.0
Carnarvon	31.4	21.0
Denbigh	30.0	23.6
Flint	29.5	23.0
Glamorgan	24.6	14.4
Merioneth	50.2	16.7
Monmouth	22.5	16.7
Montgomery	38.9	38.5
Pembroke	10.6	22.8
Radnor	28.0	26.0

Total voters registered in 1835: 34,607
Total voters registered in 1865: 44,951
Proportion of tenants-at-will in 1835: 27.6 per cent
Proportion of tenants-at-will in 1865: 24.3 per cent

(Based on 'Summary of Electoral Returns relating to Counties', P.P. 1866 LVII (3736).)

B.14 . . . Tenants at will have learnt to realize the insecurity of their tenure by very diverse but effective methods . . . Here are some instances:

1. *Eviction for exercising an independent judgment in politics*
    The *Commissioners* have received some evidence of this already. They will receive more. It will take years to forget the thrill of horror which spread through Wales, more especially through its tenantry, after the political evictions which followed the elections of 1859 and 1868. Four

uncles and relatives of mine were evicted for refusing to vote for the *Tory* candidate . . . In the election of 1865, the landlords of this district stood in this hall to watch their tenants voting, and I have heard tenants express their shame that, terrified by the evictions of 1859, they voted against their will and conscience. It was after the election of 1868 that Cardiganshire and Carnarvonshire suffered most.

(Royal Commission on Land in Wales and Monmouthshire, *Minutes of Evidence*, I, Question 16, 910. Also quoted in *Speeches and Addresses by the late Thomas E. Ellis, MP* (Wrexham, 1912), p.256.)

B.15   Sir,

The next time you send your Voting Papers to *Dowlais* please to leave them all at the *Dowlais* Office, for it will spare you and them a great deal of trouble. For the man that was distributing this time could not find out the Voters' residences because he was a stranger to the place. Then the *Dowlais* agents had to call in every house to tell the Voters who he was to vote for.

So the easiest way is the best way to accomplish everything that will answer the same purpose in the end. Therefore I beg to call your attention to the above plan, for it will answer the same purpose, and save a great deal of useless bodily exercise to both parties, and time spent without doing good. Which the late renowned Benjamin Franklyn said was money.

Wishing you success in all your endeavours, I remain yours Truly.

(A Voter: To the Merthyr Tydfil Union and Board of Health. No date (April 1853)

Sir,

I can not rest happy under the flagrant abuse of authority we suffer in the place without making our complaint known to you, as a higher power, and I suppose with power to control our movements. Will you be so kind as to inform me whether it is legal for the Iron Masters or any other party to send their agents to follow the delivery of Voting Papers dictating to the Voters how to fill them — and not only that but to fill them for them, *and* cross the names of other candidates out. The abuse here has been very great — plenty of evidence — reading and willing . . .

(John Jones, Grocer, *Dowlais*, to the General Board of Health: 7 April 1853.)

That the *Public Health Act* gives the General Board of Health no powers to supervise elections or to coerce the Local Boards into a discharge of their duties under the act.

(Tom Taylor, G[iven]B[y]H[and] to John Jones, *Dowlais*: 12 April 1853.)

(PRO MH 13/125. These documents are to be found in *Public Health in Mid-Victorian Wales. Correspondence from the Principality to the General Board of Health and Local Government Office 1848–71.* Transcribed and edited by Alun Huw Williams for the University of Wales Board of Celtic Studies (1983) *sub* Merthyr Tydfil.)

B.16   I am informed that a very close canvass is proceeding for the representation of Cardiff. My own feelings are warmly interested for the success of the Liberal Freetrade candidate, Mr Coffin, and I wish you to mention to any Tenants or Workmen of mine who may have votes, that I shall be very glad if it is consistent with their own opinions to support him. I write this because I am informed that much intimidation and undue influence is proceeding on the other side, and to prevent misrepresentations of my views. This I am told has been the case respecting Thomas John of Broviskin who rents of me, and on whom I wish you to call without delay upon the subject.

(Lady Charlotte Guest to J.H.Austin, 17 June 1851. Glamorgan Record Office, D.I.C.L.1852 (i) letter 293. Quoted in Rosemary Jones, 'The Cardiff Borough Election of 1852', M.A. (Wales), 1982.)

B.17a RETURN OF EXPENSES IN THE 1868 ELECTION

County	Candidate	Total Expenses	Numbers who Voted	Total Electors
Breconshire	G.C. Morgan	£84 3s 3d No contest		2,288
Cardiganshire	E.M. Richards	£2028 16s 9d	2,074	5,123
	E.M. Vaughan	£3152 4s 7d	1,918	
Carmarthenshire	E.J. Sartoris	£4347 9s 10d	3,280	8,026
	John Jones	£3361 12s 9d	2,942	
	H.L. Duxley	£3768 6s 9d	2,828	
	David Pugh	£2837 9s 4d	1,340	
Caernarfon	T.L.D. Jones Parry	£2427 12s 3d	1,968	4,852
	G. Douglas Pennant	£7024 8s 4d	1,815	
Denbighshire	Sir W.W. Wynn	£6980 10s 0d	3,355	7,623
	G.C. Morgan	£4311 5s 1d	2,720	
	R.M. Biddulph	£376 3s 5d	2,412	
Flintshire	Lord Richard Grosvenor	£244 1s 4d No contest		4,150
Glamorgan	C.R.M. Talbot	£62 3s 8d No contest		11,329
	H. Hussey Vivian	£162 5s 10d		
Merioneth	David Williams	£27 6s 1d No contest		3,187
	W.R.M. Wynne	£2083 6s 11d		
Monmouthshire	C.O.S. Morgan and Oulett Somerset	£11535 4s 0d	3,525	
	H.M. Clifford	£3121 16s 6d	2,338	
Montgomeryshire	C.W. Williams Wynn	£194 4s 0d No contest		4,810
Pembrokeshire	J.H. Scourfield	£207 19s 0d No contest		3,644
Radnorshire	Arthur Walsh	£2255 10s 11d No contest		2,216

Borough	Candidate	Total Expenses	Numbers who Voted	Total Electors
Beaumaris	W.O. Stanley	£553 5s 4d	941	1,944
	Morgan Lloyd	£342 10s 10d	650	
Cardiff	J.F.D. Crichton Stuart	£2917 18s 8d	2,501	5,388
	H.S. Giffard	£4796 10s 8d	2,055	
Cardigan	Sir T.D. Lloyd	£65 17s 5d No contest		1,652
Carmarthen	J.S.C. Stepney	£832 2s 11d	1,892	3,190
	M.D. Treherne	£1226 1s 11d	595	
Caernarfon	W.B. Hughes	£766 0s 0d	1,601	3,376
	T.J. Wynn	£1805 7s 4d	1,051	
Denbigh	Watkin Williams	£1914 18s 9d	1,319	2,785
	Townsend Mainwaring	£1027 7s 8d		

B.17a (cont'd)

Borough	Candidate	Total Expenses	Numbers who Voted	Total Electors
Flint	Sir John Hanmer	£599 10s 4d	No contest	3,280
Haverfordwest	William Edwardes	£1344 2s 11d	638	1,526
	Samuel Pitman	£1302 5s 7d	497	
Merthyr	Henry Richard	£512 7s 2d	11,683	14,577
	Richard Fothergill	£3058 4s 11d	7,439	
	H.A. Bruce	£1920 18s 5d	5,776	
Monmouth	Sir J.W. Ramsden	£2772 9s 11d	1,618	3,771
	Samuel Homphrey	£2591 1s 8d	1,449	
Montgomery	C.R.D. Hanbury Tracy	£101 17s 7d	No contest	2,559
Pembroke	Thomas Meyrick	£1108 12s 0d	1,419	3,028
	Sir Hugh Owen	£277 15s 11d	1,049	
Radnor	R.G. Price	£106 16s 6d	No contest	831
Swansea	L.Ll Dillwyn	£92 9s 9d	No contest	

(Abstracted from Parliamentary Papers 1868–9, L (424))

B.17b *June 27 (Dowlais)* . . . There will not now be probably any contest, the nomination is fixed for Tuesday, and everything hitherto has gone on quietly. But I regret to say that the *Chartist*s have printed and stuck up papers calling upon the working classes to attend on Tuesday in order to ask Sir John (Guest, the sitting member) to give account of former votes and to pledge himself to them for the future. This is all nonsense . . .

June 29 . . . John Evans (the manager of the Iron Works) came to fetch me, and I proceeded towards the *Vestry room* in order to take Merthyr (i.e. Sir John Guest) to the hustings . . . Before, however, I could reach that spot he met me, and told me that a *Chartist*, Argust [Francis Argust, a shoemaker], had proposed the *Chartist* leader (i.e. Morgan Williams) as a candidate and that a poll was demanded . . . Merthyr's speech was a good one, and shewed that the price of labour was not regulated by the price of corn, but by demand and by the price of iron . . . Morgan Williams made a very long and prosy speech, part Welsh, part English. . . . He was a good deal cheered, more I think than the other speakers. When he had done, his proposer Argust came forward and said that he withdrew and would not go to the Poll, after which Merthyr was duly returned.

(Lady Charlotte Guest, *Extracts from her Journal 1833–1852.* Edited by the Earl of Bessborough (1950), pp.122–24.)

B.18a NUMBERS OF ELECTORS IN 1868–9

Counties	£12 Occupiers	Other Qualifications	Total
Anglesey	857	2639	3496
Brecon	1347	2297	3644
Cardigan	1046	4069	5115
Carmarthen	2614	5412	8026
Caernarfon	1628	3224	4852
Denbigh	1971	5652	7623
Flint	1223	2927	4150
Glamorgan	2473	8856	11329
Merioneth	1132	2053	3185
Monmouth	2044	5927	7971
Montgomery	1187	3623	4810
Pembroke	1154	3536	4690
Radnor	587	1629	2216

Boroughs	Electors
Beaumaris	1944
Brecon	808
Cardigan	1561
Cardiff	5388
Carmarthen	3190
Caernarfon	3376
Denbigh	2785
Flint	3280
Haverfordwest	1526
Merthyr	14577
Monmouth	3771
Montgomery	2559
Pembroke	3028
Radnor	841
Swansea	7543

(Parliamentary Papers, 1868–9, L(418–9).)

B.18b The chairman reminded the meeting of a remark of Mr Bruce's at the hustings when a show of hands went against him. 'Ah', said he to the people, 'you may hold up your dirty hands against me, but tomorrow I'll be the member for Merthyr in spite of you'. (Cries of shame). The 'dirty' hands had got the power now and would they forget an insult of that kind?

(*Merthyr Telegraph*, 17 October 1868.)

B.19 Ballot Act (1872)
Statutes of the Realm, 35 & 36 Vict. c.33.
2. In the case of a poll at an election the votes shall be given by ballot. The ballot of each voter shall consist of a paper (in this Act called a ballot paper) showing the names and description of the candidates. Each ballot paper shall have a number printed on the back, and shall have attached a counterfoil with the same number printed on the face. At the time of voting, the ballot paper shall be marked on both sides with an official mark, and delivered to the voter within the polling station, and the number of such voter on the register of voters shall be marked on the counterfoil, and the voter having secretly marked his vote on the paper, and folded it up so as to conceal his vote, shall place it in a closed box in the presence of the officer presiding at the polling station (in this Act called 'the presiding officer') after having shown to him the official mark at the back.

Any ballot paper which has not on its back the official mark, or on which votes are given to more candidates than the voter is entitled to vote for, or on which anything, except the said number on the back, is written or marked by which the voter can be identified, shall be void and not counted.

After the close of the poll the ballot boxes shall be sealed up, so as to prevent the introduction of additional ballot papers, and shall be taken charge of by the returning officer, and that officer shall, in the presence of such agents, if any, of the candidates as may be in attendance, open the ballot boxes, and ascertain the result of the poll by counting the votes given to each candidate, and shall forthwith declare to be elected the candidates or candidate to whom the majority of votes have been given, and return their names to the Clerk of the Crown in Chancery. The decision of the returning officer as to any question arising in respect of any ballot paper shall be final, subject to reversal on petition questioning the election or return.

Wherever an equality of votes is found to exist between any candidates at an election for a county or borough, and the addition of a vote would entitle any of such candidates to be declared elected, the returning officer, if a registered elector of such county or borough, may give such additional vote, but shall not in any other case be entitled to vote at an election for which he is returning officer.

Debating the Evidence

Professor Ieuan Gwynedd Jones's essay examines the comparatively placid and traditional forms of organized political activity in the mid-nineteenth century. He, too, draws heavily on evidence from newspapers and official government and parliamentary enquiries. In particular, Professor Jones's use of statistical evidence is worth noting. The appearance of material such as census data and electoral returns reflect greater government interest and involvement in society in the nineteenth century. Compared to the subjective nature of evidence given by informants to Royal Commissions, for example, are we dealing with accurate and objective facts? We shall see below that this is not the case. Professor Jones also makes use of the records of political organizations (the *National Reform Union*, the *National Reform League*, the *Anti-Corn Law League*, the Liberation Society) and of the writings of leading political radicals such as *Henry Richard* and Thomas Rees. We have a mixture here of official or organizational records and of what are sometimes called *polemical* sources, i.e. sources which overtly display conviction, an articulated political philosophy and a deliberate attempt to persuade in a one-sided way. By their very nature these are subjective and biased. This does not mean that they are of no use. Finally, Ieuan Gwynedd Jones's use of an extract from a personal diary — the journal of Lady Charlotte Guest — is also noteworthy. Perhaps after the stolid diet of official material and the spice of polemic, we have here a direct and immediate human testimony. However, the problem of the typicality of such material — let alone its subjectivity — is significant.

Source B.1

What does this document tell us about contemporary attitudes to Wales and Welsh nationalism?

Source B.2

As the author considers the degree of support for universal *suffrage* at this time, what do you think might be the weakness of this source? What comment made by Professor Jones in this article needs to be considered in this respect?

Source B.3

In considering the strength of political opinion in favour of Parliamentary reform, what would you need to know about the *National Reform League* in making use of this source?

Source B.4

Given the objective set out in document (a), what does document (b) reveal about the work of the Liberation Society in Wales between 1861 and 1866? In what way does Source B.9 support document (b) here?

Source B.5

In view of the evidence in Sources D and E, what do you make of the first sentence in this source? Given the authorship of the source what do you make of its reliability as evidence?

Source B.6

What claim made here about the attitude of Welsh people to politics seems to support the evidence in Source B.5? What is there here which may enlighten us as to the value of newspaper evidence?

Source B.7

What is your view of this as a possible source for the study of the *Scotch Cattle* and *Chartism* in Wales? Compare this source to Source E.2 — which do you think is the more reliable evidence for support for the *Scotch Cattle* and *Chartism* in Wales? For what historical question is this primary evidence?

Source B.8

From evidence you read in Source E do you agree with the claim in this source that 'there have been only two considerable exceptions to this rule'? From your reading of Source D what comment would you make on *Henry Richard*'s claims as to the causes of the Rebecca riots?

Source B.9
This evidence is from the Census of Religious Worship in England and Wales, 1851. The calculations here are based on a count of the number of people attending places of worship on a particular Sunday. What questions might you need to ask in interpreting this evidence? How reliable is such information as a guide to the religious beliefs and affiliations of the Welsh people of this time?

Source B.10
What does this source show about the attitude of Welsh MPs? How do you think this evidence was obtained and how might it be checked?

Source B.11
What does this source show? Compare and explain the differences in the percentages in the county franchise table for north and south Wales and those for Haverfordwest and Cardiff in the borough table.

Source B.12
What does a comparison between the percentage of working-class electors in Pembroke and Merthyr at this time reveal?

Source B.13
Who were tenants-at-will? Why did they form a much greater percentage of the electorate in a county like Merioneth compared to Glamorgan? What significance did this differentiation have for Welsh politics?

Source B.14
What are the strengths and weaknesses of this source?

Source B.15
What is the writer of the first letter here saying and why does he write in the style that he does? Why do you think he chooses to be anonymous? In what way does the evidence in the second letter support that in the first?

Source B.16
In what way does the evidence here support that in B.15? Which of the two sources do you consider to be the more reliable and revealing?

Source B.17a
What additional information would help to make this evidence on contested elections more useful? How reliable is this document?

Source B.17b
What particular words or phrases here do you feel reveal Lady Charlotte Guest's attitude towards *Chartism*?

Source B.18a
Compare the information in this source on the number of voters in boroughs, with that in Source B.12. What is the overall trend and how do you explain this? Where do the biggest numerical increases take place and what might be the explanation for this?

Source B.18b
What does the reference to 'dirty hands' in this source mean and what is its significance?

Source B.19
Given the evidence contained in Sources B.14, B.15 and B.16, what was likely to be the effect of the Ballot Act?

Discussion

The questions posed on polemical sources (such as B.5, B.7, B.8) are intended to demonstrate the wariness with which the historian must treat such sources. *Henry Richard* was a leading *Nonconformist* and Radical — a prominent figure in the Liberation Society and MP for Merthyr Tydfil after 1868. Thomas Rees was a leading *Nonconformist* minister and an historian of the movement. How well placed were they to provide reliable evidence on Rebecca and *Chartism*? Certainly, they lived through the period of these movements and may well have had direct experience of them. However, their commentary is much more that of the historian or the polemicist than of the direct observer. Their views are in essence secondary interpretations rather than primary sources. This does not mean that we can dismiss their evidence. The strength of this type of source lies in what it reveals about the attitudes of radical Liberals and *Nonconformists* in nineteenth-century Wales. These were prominent men. Their comments are noteworthy.

The historian also has to be careful with statistics. Whilst some sources (B.10, B.11, B.12, B.13, B.18a) appear to be straightforward in the evidence they offer and the interpretation they suggest, and can be cross-checked for accuracy, other examples of statistical evidence are far more problematic. Source B.17a is presumably based on returns made to the authorities by candidates or their agents, which have then been collated by Parliamentary officials. To what extent does this allow an accurate picture to emerge of the role which money played in deciding Parliamentary elections? For example, would the expenses presumably incurred by John Austin at the behest of Lady Charlotte Guest (B.16) be shown in such official returns? How can we be certain that in direct and indirect ways, money was not covertly used to decide the outcome? In any event, is money the only form of influence brought to bear in such situations? Source B.9 is another example of the problems encountered in handling statistical evidence. The Census of Religious Worship of 1851, whilst being a unique indication of the strength and spread of religious affiliation in the nineteenth century, is a source which has long caused problems for historians. For example, in the indexes at the foot of B.9 the population of Wales in 1851 and the total attendances at places of worship on 'Census Sunday' in that year, are given. The obvious inference is that a very high percentage of the population in Wales attended a church or chapel on that day. Such an interpretation would be totally misleading. Attendance figures are actually an *aggregate* of total attendances on 'Census Sunday' and we know for certain that many people attended more than one service on that day. The overall percentage of the population attending any service was therefore much lower than is suggested here. This is not to devalue the importance of the *Religious Census* to historians and the possibilities it offers for generalizing about Welsh religious affiliations in 1851, but it does reveal that statistics can seriously mislead as well as inform.

Capel Newydd Nanhoron, Llŷn. Built in 1770. (*Source: National Monuments Record for Wales.*)

The Nonconformist Response

CHRISTOPHER TURNER

By any test *Nonconformity* was a powerful and pervasive force in nineteenth-century Wales. The chapels of the main denominations dominated almost every town and village, except perhaps in those places so near to the English border as to render them beyond redemption. Historians have argued over whether statistics can be regarded as true indices to religious practice, but the unique experiment of the *Religious Census of 1851*, despite the contemporary controversy which surrounded it, at least gave some quantitative support to *Nonconformist* claims of superiority over the Church. For *Henry Richard*, the Liberal *Nonconformist*, it also proved, if such proof were needed, that Wales was fundamentally a more religious nation than England (C.1).

C.1

The Census provided a wealth of detailed information but perhaps the most reliable data relate to the 'sittings' provided by the various religious groups. In other words, it established how many people could be accommodated in each church or chapel. Horace Mann, who was responsible for the report which resulted from the census, devised a statistical test by which he estimated that to be minimally effective the churches should make provision for 58.4 per cent of the population in each region. This figure was easily achieved by all the registration counties of Wales, while Caernarfonshire could accommodate an enviable 94 per cent of its total population (C.2). Even at the level of the registration district the figure of 57.9 per cent for Merthyr Tydfil, for many Welshmen a byword for irreligion, compared very favourably with the 31.6 per cent recorded by Manchester. This variation pointed to one of the major

C.2

differences between Wales and England, for in the industrial areas of Wales religious provision continued to be demanded, whilst in England it appeared that industrialism was accompanied by a pronounced lack of interest in religious worship (C.3). The *Nonconformists* conveniently ignored the existence in Wales of a significant, if minority, section of the population which never attended any place of worship.

    The Census also showed that both traditional Dissent, in the shape of the *Baptists* and *Independents*, and the *Methodist* groups which emerged from the eighteenth-century revival, had assumed positions of considerable strength by 1851. The most representative of the Welsh denominations were the *Calvinistic Methodists*. In four counties they provided more accommodation than the *Established Church* and it is significant that these counties (Cardiganshire, Merioneth, Caernarfonshire, and Anglesey) were precisely those which were furthest from English influence. They were then and have remained the bastions of the Welsh language. The *Baptist* and *Independent* strongholds were in south Wales but the *Calvinistic Methodists*, whilst they could claim some influence throughout Wales, had a virtual hegemony in the north.

    Another useful and non-controversial aspect of the *Religious Census* was the listing of dates of chapel erection or enlargement. Given the absence of reliable figures relating to chapel membership, an analysis of building dates allows a chronology of growth to be devised (C.4). The period 1801–51 reveals a pattern of unrestricted expansion. Within this pattern there were years of particular growth and usually, though not exclusively, these were periods of religious revival. In the first half of the century revivals seemed to occur with commendable regularity towards the end of each decade. It was the revival or 'season of spiritual refreshment' which nourished Welsh congregations in two ways. Firstly, revivals preserved the future of the congregation by drawing more people under its direct control, either by attracting new members or, more likely, by converting those who already attended as 'hearers' (gwrandawyr) into full members. Secondly, revivals continually injected a new spiritual awareness into those who already habitually attended (C.5).

C.3

C.4

C.5

Nonconformist expansion continued into the second half of the century although perhaps not to the same extent as it had done previously. Membership figures are more reliable after 1860 and by expressing the annual increase or decrease in membership as a percentage of the previous year's total (growth rate) a

C.6   reasonably accurate pattern can be compiled (C.6). Again, revivals in 1859 and 1904 played their part in maintaining *Nonconformist* strength in the short term. Inevitably, it became harder to expand as the rate of population growth increased. The population of Wales increased by 45 per cent between 1861 and 1891. Yet even to retain membership levels at a time when non-Welsh immigration was increasing in the industrial areas, and there was a steady depopulation in rural areas, was a tribute to the exertions of the denominations themselves.

Contemporary observers offered a range of diverse opinions as to why *Nonconformity* had been so successful. The Education *Commissioners* who presented the 'treacherous' *Blue Books of 1847*, whilst they failed to comprehend the values of an alien culture,

C.7   did perceive the popular appeal of Welsh *Nonconformity* (C.7). Similarly, the social survey undertaken by the pioneering English newpaper, the *Morning Chronicle*, pointed to the lack of class distinction between minister and congregation as one reason for *Nonconformist* success in the industrial areas of south

C.8   Wales (C.8). The *Nonconformists* themselves, like the *Independent* minister, the Revd Evan Jones (Ieuan Gwynedd), were stung into action by the *Blue Books* controversy and they preferred to explain their success in terms of the previous neglect shown by

C.9   the Established Church (C.9). Other *Nonconformist* apologists cited powerful preaching in the Welsh language and the particular work of the *Sunday School* as important contributions. Equally, as the evangelical vicar of Aberdare, the Revd John Griffith, realized, it was the decentralized nature of *Nonconformity* which allowed it to erect its chapels in the midst of new communities, which gave it a distinct advantage over the outdated parochial system of the Church, especially in the

C.10   industrial districts (C.10).

But such statements do not provide the complete answer. For example, they beg the question as to why an expansive, democratic and, in later political terms, radical movement should have appeared to be so totally opposed to workers' attempts to improve their condition. Generally, the Welsh denominations were wholly conservative in outlook. They were unanimous in their opposition to the early trade unions, viewing them as contrary to the true spirit of Christianity. The *Calvinistic Methodists* in 1832 threatened all union members with

C.11 excommunication (C.11). Similarly, they were horrified at the excesses of *Chartism* and, whilst sympathizing with the aims of the Rebecca rioters, very few ministers would condone the attack on property and associated acts of violence. Of all the Welsh denominations, the *Calvinistic Methodists* seemed always prepared to speak out against anything which resembled a challenge to established authority. The undisputed leader of the *Methodists* in the 1830s was John Elias and he issued a strident condemnation of *Chartism*, seeing it as an offence against the

C.12 constitution and proper government of the country (C.12).

Later in the 1860s the arguments against *unionism* and strikes were expressed differently but the end result was the same. The influential *Baptist* leader, the Revd Thomas Price of Aberdare, urged the colliers in his area to maintain harmonious relations with the coalowners at all costs. He was adamant that strikes would only harm the interests of the workmen themselves and

C.13 he could see no benefit in forming a union (C.13). To the workmen he may have become too closely identified with local colliery owners, with whom he worked on political matters, to be taken too seriously, though his political leadership remained unchallenged. Price's views were shared by the *Calvinistic Methodists* who opposed trade unions on theological grounds. For them Calvinism stressed the need to attain individual salvation by faith alone. It therefore seemed incongruous that workmen should join a union which, by definition, undermined the freedom of action and independence of the individual. The standard *Nonconformist* view was that trade *unionism*, like *Chartism*, was imported from England and was, therefore, not suited to the particular character of the God-fearing Welshman

C.14 (C.14). Because centralized control was less pronounced in the *Baptist* denomination, and certainly amongst the *Independents*, a few individual ministers and their congregations might have offered support to certain protest movements. During a strike at Aberdare in 1850 the *Cardiff and Merthyr Guardian* reported the 'shameful' action of one local chapel which excommunicated those of its members who returned to work before the strike was over. But this was not typical and other ministers were quick to disassociate themselves from such action (C.15).

C.15

Generally, the denominations seemed unable to give a lead to the working classes in social matters. The standard response to unemployment, extreme poverty, death and disease was largely negative. They expressed genuine sympathy for the workers' plight but the advice was to accept such 'worldly' problems as divinely ordained. The consolation they offered was that, despite present circumstance, through constant faith they might achieve ultimate salvation. The *Baptists*, for example, believed that the true Christian was 'called out of this world' and should therefore stand aloof from an overriding interest in the problems of the present (C.16). As proof of this 'otherworldliness' *Nonconformity* sought to introduce vigorous tests of faith, especially in the form of the temperance, or total abstinence, pledge (C.17). The predominant view was that poverty was the result of intemperate habits, and this remained the case even at the end of the century (C.18).

C.16

C.17

C.18

Some historians have argued that this kind of religious self-discipline was in reality a form of social control by which working men could be subdued and prevented from challenging the existing class system. There is little doubt that colliery officials, for example, were not blind to the moralizing effects of religion on their workers and on those who were unemployed (C.19). The lessons of temperance, thrift and obedience to authority tended to improve output by producing a more sober, hard-working and malleable work force. In return employers of labour would often support the denominations by contributing to chapel building and sponsoring their various functions (C.20).

C.19

C.20

But to view Welsh *Nonconformity* simply as an agent of repression would be to deny its essential populism. During its formative years it was unarguably a movement from below. Chapels became the means by which ordinary people organized their lives. They were social centres providing access to literary and musical entertainments, at first through hymn singing but

Kindred spirits? Aberdare. (*Source: Cynon Valley Libraries.*)

CONTENTS.

ARROWS

FROM A

TEMPERANCE QUIVER.

BY THE

REV. JOSEPH EVANS,

CARMARTHEN.

LONDON:

JOHN KEMPSTER & Co., 9 & 10, ST. BRIDE'S AVENUE, FLEET STREET, E.C.

CARMARTHEN: W. E. JONES, CHEMIST, DARK-GATE.

later through the performance of classical choral works. Above all else, the chapels provided the means by which the Welsh people attempted to educate themselves. The role of the *Sunday Schools* in providing basic education was universally acknowledged. Many people were able to read and write directly as a result of the instruction they received at *Sunday School* (C.21). Chapel organization also taught the basic elements of self-government and provided instruction in 'keeping the books'. In essence, the chapels provided ordinary people with a means of expression, irrespective of the narrow theological content, in their own language (C.22).

C.21

C.22

It is certainly possible to understand why *Nonconformity* opposed most of the radical movements of the first half of the nineteenth century. For much of the time it was concerned first with its own existence in the difficult years during and after the *Napoleonic Wars*, and later with its perpetual struggle to achieve legal equality with the *Established Church*. The dominant questions were those of *Church rates*, burial rights, *tithes*, marriage rights, education and the culmination of all these, *Disestablishment*. It was rarely concerned with social issues affecting the industrial communities except where these were likely to affect, in a detrimental way, its own pursuit of equality and freedom of action.

In one important sense the rapid growth of *Nonconformity* was in itself a response to industrialization. In Wales, as in America, an expansionist and enthusiastic religion was to provide a source of comfort to a society which was experiencing a fundamental transformation involving different living conditions, new patterns of work and a revised set of social (class) relations.

It achieved this largely by deflecting the problems of this world into an all-embracing search for salvation in the next. To counteract the fear of death underground, for example, prayer meetings were often held before the start of the day's work. This happened particularly during revivals and was not confined to the collieries of the south but also occurred in the slate caverns of the north and the lead mines of mid-Wales (C.23). The pursuit of this 'social security' offered by *Noncon-*

C.23

formity was at its most hectic during revivals and these tended to occur when social problems were at their worst. Again, the Revd John Griffith, unlike his *Nonconformist* contemporaries, was not afraid to point out that there was more than the hand of

C.24 God in these displays of religious enthusiasm (C.24). *Nonconformist* ministers actually played on social tension and fear in order to terrify their congregations into a dramatic realization of sin and the need for immediate repentance. The 'Cholera' revivals of 1832 and 1849 (so called because these religious revivals were stimulated by cholera outbreaks) provide good examples whereby ministers were able to use the understand-

C.25 able forebodings of their congregations to best effect (C.25).

Nonconformity therefore provided an outlet for tension and an escape from drudgery and fear. It put into a more acceptable perspective the harsh realities of industrial existence. But *Nonconformity* could perform this role only because it was already an established fact of Welsh life. The people who flooded into the industrial areas up to the 1870s were Welsh people, usually from neighbouring rural counties, who brought

C.26 their faith with them (C.26). The establishment of *Nonconformity* in the newly formed industrial areas must be seen therefore as the successful transplantation of a rural religion into an industrial environment. The first action of immigrants to the iron and coal towns was to find a suitable place of worship. The substantial effort involved in obtaining a site, building a chapel and paying off the subsequent debt was the outward sign of a community resisting change. For these were people who refused to acquiesce in the forces of 'progress' and become an industrial society overnight.

Yet it was the very success of *Nonconformity* which was to present problems later in the century. By the 1890s the denominations themselves were beginning to question whether their earlier success had produced a feeling of complacency and

C.27 over-emphasized respectability (C.27). The political victory of 1868 and the closer association with Liberalism were major successes but they were not achieved without some cost to the 'other-worldly' principles on which *Nonconformity* had been founded. In 1890 the Revd James Owen (*Baptist*) called on *Nonconformists* to participate in local and national politics as a

Revd Christmas Evans, aged 59, in 1835. (*Source: National Library of Wales.*)

C.28   natural concomitant to religious worship. Such a view would have been unthinkable in the earlier period (C.28). It was inevitable that *Nonconformity* would contribute towards the emergence of a Welsh middle class because of its constant teaching of thrift and self-help. Many of the skills needed to run a business could be learnt as a deacon in the local chapel. The Commission which reported on religion in Wales in 1910 looked back at the way in which the economy and religious C.29   practice of Wrexham developed in parallel (C.29). In this way the stabilization of Welsh society in the second phase of industrialization after 1860 was matched by a stabilization within the denominations themselves. An example of this was the greater emphasis on ministerial training and the consequent rise in status which this brought to *Nonconformist* ministers C.30   (C.30).

The most visible sign that *Nonconformity* had achieved its maturity was the physical appearance of chapels themselves. The *Independent* historian, the Revd Thomas Rees, welcomed the erection of ornate and imposing chapels as 'ornaments to the locality' and he blamed the primitive structures of the earlier C.31   period not so much on poverty as on a lack of vision (C.31).

Greater self-confidence also brought a change in outlook. The denominations increasingly turned their attention away from the revitalization of their own congregations, an essential facet of earlier revivals, and towards the conversion of the unbeliever. This was especially the case in the larger Welsh towns where immigration had brought in a large number of non-Welsh people whose apparent custom it was, according to the *Nonconformists*, never to attend places of worship. The provision of English-language services for such people caused much debate within the denominations. The dominant opinion was that the Welsh language should not be preserved at the expense of the greater principles of religion and morality but some believed, with equal conviction, that true religion was C.32   only capable of being taught in the Welsh language (C.32). The Revd D. Evans in his *The Sunday Schools of Wales*, published in 1884, summed up the problem when he described the role of the Welsh language in the *Sunday Schools*. For him, the study of Welsh was essential not so much because of the need to preserve

the language but because it was the best means of raising
C.33   spirituality (C.33).

In the last two decades of the century there is evidence that
some working people began to resent what they perceived as a
C.34   move away from the original ideals of *Nonconformity* (C.34).
Such critics pointed to the current practice of appointing
deacons not for their spiritual gifts but simply because they had
C.35   some measure of influence in the outside world (C.35). It is
probable that individuals from the working classes did forsake
chapel attendance and move towards a more active interest in
trade *unionism* and later, socialism. But the retention of chapel
membership levels in the 1880s suggested that a large proportion of the working classes, despite the opposition (or at best
neutrality) of the denominations during industrial disputes, did
not see *Nonconformity* and *unionism* as mutually exclusive.

When *Nonconformity* finally yielded to the secularist side of
the twentieth century it was the irresistible advance of English
C.36   immigration into the industrial areas which was to blame (C.36).
The antagonism of the denominations towards working-class
movements, radical Liberalism apart, must have influenced
some individuals to withdraw from organized religion but, for
at least a generation after the momentous 1904/5 revival,
Nonconformity continued to represent a body of Welsh opinion
which it was difficult to ignore.

Sources

C.1   From these facts there are some inferences that are obvious and
irresistible. They prove — First, that the Church of England is
not the Church of Wales. Secondly, that but for the exertions of
the *Nonconformists*, Wales would have been at this time, as
regards its spiritual interests in a most pitiable plight. A most
estimable clergyman, a native of Wales, whose name is still
venerated by many in this metropolis, the Revd Williams
Howels, of Long Acre, once said, that but for the *Methodists* and
Dissenters, the devil might long ere this have claimed the
Principality as his own special diocese. Thirdly, that the

voluntary principle, when fairly worked, is sufficient to supply the spiritual wants of a nation, seeing that the Welsh, amid poverty, isolation, and discouragement, have provided themselves with more ample means of religious worship and instruction than can be found, perhaps, among any people under the face of heaven.

(Henry Richard, *Letters on the Social and Political Condition of Wales*, 1866, pp.22–23.)

C.2   See page 86.

C.3   While it appears that the bulk of the working classes of England never attend the means of grace, and that a large proportion of them are avowed infidels, fully ninety per cent of the corresponding classes in Wales regularly attend public worship, except in the large towns and most Anglicized districts, and even in those localities at least seventy-five per cent of the Welsh-speaking masses are frequent or constant attendants at one or the other of our places of worship. A century ago our working classes were quite as irreligious as those classes are now in England, and incomparably more ignorant, but in the present day they are under the influence of religion to a far greater extent than the other classes of the community. As you are now endeavouring in England to solve the problem, how the working classes are to be won to religion, which has long been happily solved in Wales, it cannot fail to be interesting to you to know by what means we have attained the object which you wish to compass.

(Revd Thomas Rees, 'The Working Classes of Wales and Religious Institutions', in *Miscellaneous Papers relating to Wales*, 1867, p.24.)

C.2 NUMBER OF SITTINGS PROVIDED BY THE WELSH DENOMINATIONS—1851

COUNTY	CHURCH OF ENGLAND		INDEPENDENTS		BAPTISTS		WESLEYAN METHODISTS		CALVINISTIC METHODISTS		TOTAL	
Monmouthshire Popn: 177,130	39,215	22.1 %	14,135	8.0 %	28,377	16.0 %	16,606	9.4 %	7,179	4.1 %	116,266	65.6 %
Glamorgan Popn: 240,095	39,324	16.4 %	38,378	16.0 %	30,475	12.7 %	11,902	4.9 %	27,921	11.6 %	152,088	63.3 %
Carmarthenshire Popn: 94,672	22,321	23.6 %	20,088	21.2 %	9,785	10.3 %	3,757	4.0 %	14,399	15.2 %	70,976	75.0 %
Pembrokeshire Popn: 84,472	25,367	30.0 %	14,323	16.9 %	13,125	15.5 %	6,909	8.2 %	5,701	6.7 %	67,004	79.3 %
Cardiganshire Popn: 97,614	21,569	22.1 %	15,267	15.6 %	11,291	11.5 %	3,666	3.7 %	22,053	22.6 %	82,335	84.3 %
Brecknockshire Popn: 59,178	17,842	30.1 %	9,892	16.7 %	8,739	14.8 %	3,840	6.5 %	6,733	11.4 %	48,746	82.4 %
Radnorshire Popn: 31,425	13,204	42.0 %	2,102	6.7 %	3,165	10.1 %	1,731	5.5 %	1,385	4.4 %	22,802	72.6 %
Montgomeryshire Popn: 77,142	22,362	29.0 %	9,910	12.8 %	4,167	5.4 %	10,481	13.6 %	12,796	16.6 %	62,886	81.5 %
Flintshire Popn: 41,047	10,660	26.0 %	4,933	12.0 %	1,402	3.4 %	6,749	16.4 %	6,542	15.9 %	32,177	78.4 %
Denbighshire Popn: 96,915	36,535	31.5 %	10,507	10.8 %	7,235	7.5 %	11,872	12.2 %	25,921	26.7 %	91,177	94.0 %
Merionethshire Popn: 51,307	8,895	17.3 %	7,212	14.0 %	1,934	3.8 %	3,299	6.4 %	13,550	26.4 %	35,161	68.3 %
Caernarfonshire Popn: 94,674	24,096	25.4 %	12,892	13.6 %	4,786	5.0 %	9,207	9.7 %	38,284	40.4 %	85,199	90.0 %
Anglesey Popn: 43,243	8,654	20.0 %	4,606	10.6 %	2,718	6.3 %	2,506	5.8 %	12,912	29.8 %	31,725	73.4 %

(Census of Religious Worship 1851. Report and Tables, 1853, pp.120–129.)

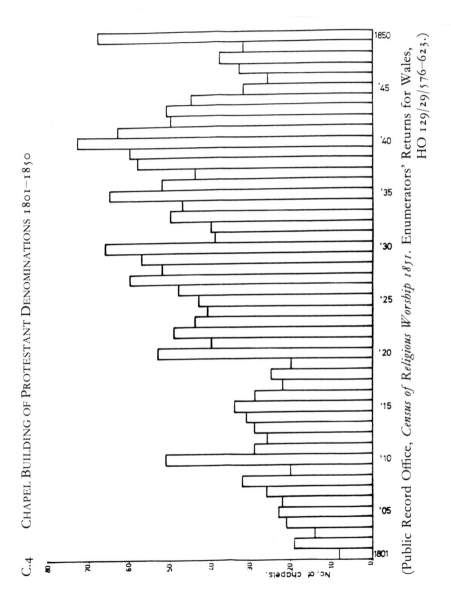

C.4   CHAPEL BUILDING OF PROTESTANT DENOMINATIONS 1801–1850

(Public Record Office, *Census of Religious Worship 1851*. Enumerators' Returns for Wales, HO 129/29/576–623.)

C.5   I heard Mr Griffiths (Llanharan), the minister, say that the reviving influence appeared too weak to move the old swearers and inveterate sinners, and that he compared the children to 'steam tugs' sent out to draw large vessels into port. After this such a power was experienced as to move the hardest and the worst of sinners. Those who were mere attendants at the sanctuary joined the Church, and others who never attended any place of worship flocked to it. The effects of the Gospel on these, hitherto strangers to it, were most wonderful. To them it *was* new — a new power, a new world; not having hardened their ears by listlessly hearing without believing, they surrendered themselves gladly, wholly, to the Saviour. Drunkards and swearers have been transformed into sober and praying people.

(Evan Davies, *Revival in Wales*, 1859, p.17.)

C.6   GROWTH RATES IN WALES — (4 MAIN DENOMINATIONS)

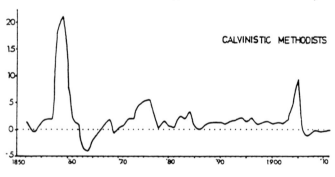

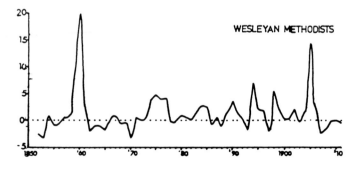

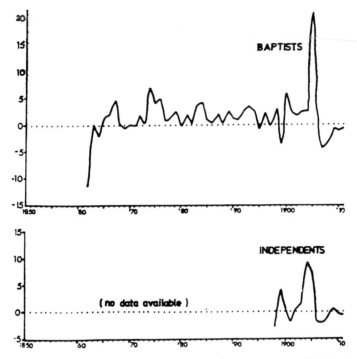

(*Y Dyddiadur*, 1850–1867, *Y Blwyddiadur*, 1867–1910 (Calvinistic Methodists); *Minutes of Evidence*, 1850–1910 (Wesleyan Methodists); *Baptist Handbook*, 1863–1910 (Baptists); *Congregational Year Book*, 1891–1910 (Independents).)

C.7   Thus his social sphere becomes one of complete isolation from all influences, save such as arise within his own order . . . He is left to live in an under-world of his own, and the march of society goes on so completely over his head, that he is never heard of, excepting when the strange and abnormal features of a Revival, or a Rebecca or *Chartist* outbreak, call attention to a phase of society which could produce anything so contrary to all that we elsewhere experience.

Cut off from, or limited to a purely material agency in, the practical world, his mental faculties, so far as they are not engrossed by the hardships of rustic, or the intemperance of manufacturing, life, have hitherto been exerted almost exclusively upon theological ideas. In this direction too, from causes which it is out of my province to particularize, he has moved under the same isolating destiny, and his worship, like his life, has grown different from that of the classes over him. Nor has he failed of tangible results in his chosen province of independent exertion. He has raised the buildings, and maintains the ministry of his worship over the whole face of his country, to an extent adequate to his accommodation.

(*Report of the Commissioners of Inquiry into the State of Education in Wales.* 1847, vol.I., p.3.)

C.8   Many of the preachers are wholly uneducated men — that is to say, their learning extends no further than to simple reading and writing. Some of them — indeed, I may say many of them— were, at the outset of life, daily labourers, like the classes whom they now lead. I was told that there were more miners in the dissenting ministry than any other class of workmen. But zeal, earnestness, and energy of character supply the place of educational acquirements with the rude, untutored masses who are here to be worked upon. The preacher who has himself been a labourer knows best the labourer's nature, and adopts the most likely means of affecting and ruling it. There is a world of native eloquence in their sermons; they are, in consonance with the genius of the Welsh language, abundantly figurative; and the preacher himself, unaccustomed to close reasoning,which would indeed be ill-adapted to his audience, appeals more to the feeling than the understanding. He affects the heart, which he can touch — and not the head, which is above him and beyond his reach. The sight of one of these huge meeting houses during service is memorable. Next to the violent and rude gesticulation of the preacher, as in a sonorous and guttural language he denounces, expostulates, persuades, and comforts, one is struck first with the vast throng of cleanly and well-dressed people that literally fills the chapel, and in the next place with the circumstances that they express sympathy with the sentiments of the discourse or prayer by ejaculations, and sometimes groans. The effect upon a stranger, accustomed to the well-trained congregations of England where there are no such audible expressions of emotion, is peculiar.

(*Morning Chronicle*, 15 April 1850.)

C.9   The truth is, that Welsh Dissent is neither more nor less than a simple contrivance to supply the spiritual wants of the Welsh people. Religion had died out from the Church; and the spiritual nature of men sought and found it in the meeting-house. It was not Church government or doctrine that caused Dissent, but the total absence of living, practical piety within the pale of national institutions.

(Revd Evan Jones (Ieuan Gwynedd), *Facts, Figures, and Statements in Illustration of the Dissent and Morality of Wales*, 1847, p.11.)

C.10   The reason of it is because it is impossible to expect that two clergymen resident among 12,000 people, scattered over a space of ten miles long by about six miles broad, can ever hope to have that hold on the parishioners which is necessary before they can be restored again to the Church.

(National Library of Wales, Church in Wales Records, LL/QA/35, 1848. Evidence of Revd John Griffith of Aberdare.)

C.11   *Penderfyniadau*

1.   Nad ydym mewn un modd yn cymeradwyo Cymdeithas undeb y Glo-wyr, Mwn-gloddwyr, a Thanwyr; oblegid yr amcan sydd ynddynt i gyrhaedd y llywyddiaeth, y dull y derbynir iddynt, y dirgelwch sydd ynddynt, ynghyd a'r dial a ddangosir at y rhai nad ydynt yn aelodau ohonynt.

2.   Fod y Corph yn tosturio wrth y rhai sydd yn aelodau ohonynt.

3.   Am bwy bynag a fyno fod yn aelod o'r gyfryw gymdeithas, na ellir mewn un modd ei oddef yn aelod eglwysig, oblegid fod y cyfryw gymdeithasau yn hollol wrthwyneb i air Duw, ac i gyfreithiau y wladwriaeth yr ydym yn ddeiliaid ynddi, yr ydym yn penderfynu eu diarddel o'n plith.

4.   Nad ydym yn dewis bod yn fyrbwyll yn y cerydd eglwysig

ar y rhai sydd yn barod wedi ymuno a'r cyfryw gymdeithasau gan y gallai rhai wneuthur hyny mewn pro-
fedigaeth ac anwybod.

5. Yr ydym yn annog pawb sydd yn aelodau ohonynt i
ymryddhau mor fuan ag y gallont. Ac er mwyn dangos
pob tiriondeb a chydymdeimlad ag amryfusedd, yr ydym
yn penderfynu diwedd mis Ebrill, a dim ymhellach: erbyn
yr hwn amser y bydd raid eu bod oll wedi ymryddhau, neu
fod yn amddifaid o ein breintiau eglwysig.

6. Na dderbynir mwyach NEB yn aelodau i'r corph hwn a
fyddont yn perthynu i'r cyfryw gymdeithasau.

7. Fod i'r Cyfarfodydd Misol, perthynol i'r Enwad crefyddol
hwn, weithredu y penderfyniadau hyn yn brydlawn a
diduedd.

(Declarations

1. That we in no way approve of the Association of the union
of the Colliers, Quarrymen and the Furnace men, because
of their intention to obtain leadership, the way in which it
is joined, the mystery surrounding them and the revenge
against those who are not members.

2. That the Body (the denomination) sympathizes with those
who are members of them.

3. Whoever wishes to be a member of such a society, cannot
be tolerated as a Church member, because such societies
are contradictory to the word of God and to the laws of
the country in which we live, and we excommunicate
them.

4. We do not choose that the Church be impulsive in
condemning those who have already joined such societies,
as some could do when in trouble or in ignorance.

5. We encourage everyone who is a member to withdraw as
soon as possible. And in order to show leniency and
consideration towards such an error, we have decided
upon the end of April, and no later: by this time all should
have withdrawn or be bereft of our church privileges.

6. That NO ONE will forthwith be accepted as members of
this body should they belong to such societies.

7. That the Monthly Meeting of this religious denomination

carry out these declarations in a prompt and impartial manner.)

(*Y Drysorfa*, 1832, p. 121.)

C.12 I am sorry to find that Infidels swarm in your towns and populous places in England. Alas, we cannot boast of the morality, quietness, and peaceable disposition of the Welsh lately, especially in some parts. The disturbance at Newport will be a lasting stain on our character. Welshmen, alas, condemned for high treason! — I was so anxious to know how our friends, the *Calvinistic Methodists*, conducted themselves in that part of the country at the time, that I wrote there to enquire; and I had the satisfaction to find that their conduct was proper and Christian-like.

(E. Morgan, *Valuable Letters, Essays and other Papers of the late Reverend John Elias of Anglesea*, 1847, p. 196.)

C.13 Un gair at weithwyr y Gadlys. Gyfeillion caredig — Yr ydych chwi yn awr yn sefyll yn uchel — yn uchel iawn fel dynion moesol, sobr, a chrefyddol — cadwch eich cymeriad a'ch enw da. Er mwyn Mr Davies, er mwyn eich meistri, ac er mwyn eich hunain, cadwch y safle ag ydych wedi ei gyrhaedd. Dyma ein gobaith, a dyma ein dymuniad ar eich rhan.

(One word to the workmen of Gadlys. Kind friends — you now stand high — very high as moral, sober and religious men — keep your character and your good name. For the sake of Mr Davies (David Davies, coalowner), for your masters' sake and your own, keep the standard you have attained. That is our hope and our desire on your behalf.)

(*Seren Cymru*, 4 September 1863.)

Y mae dros flwyddyn wedi myned heibio er pan ddarfu i ni dynu gwg llawer o'r glowyr, yn herwydd i ni yn mis Medi, 1863, roddi ein 'Gair o Ocheliad' o berthynas i flaenoriaid y mudiad o sefydlu Cymdeithas Genedlaethol i lowyr Prydain Fawr. Darfu i ni, mewn iaith eglur a digamsyniol, gondemnio y blaenoriaid fel dynion anaddas i arwain corff mawr ein gweithwyr . . . Mae y

93

flwyddyn hon wedi mwy na gwireddu pob gair a ysgrifenwyd genym yn *Seren Cymru*; ac er prawf o hyn, caiff ein gelynion fod yn farnwyr, ie, y dynion fuont mor ddiwyd yn ein cablu flwyddyn yn ol, y rhai hyn yn awr a gant lefaru am y dynion a gondemniwyd genym ni cyn iddynt hwy agor eu llygaid.

(Over a year has passed since we offended many of the miners with our 'Word of Warning' in September 1863 about the leaders of the movement to establish a National Society for the miners of Great Britain. We condemned those leaders in clear and unambiguous terms as men unfit to lead the mass of our working men . . . This year has more than confirmed every word we wrote in *Seren Cymru*. As a proof of this, let our enemies — those who disparaged us so sedulously a year ago — be the judges. Let them now speak of the men whom we condemned while their own eyes remained unopened.)

(*Seren Cymru*, 4 September and 16 December 1864.)

C.14   But has it never struck you, that *Chartism* was imported from England, that it spread chiefly among anglicized Welshmen as far as Wales was concerned, and that two out of the three leaders in the attack upon the Westgate Hotel at Newport were Englishmen? Need I remind you that the Rebecca Riots originated on account of the illegal conduct of the Aristocracy, Magistrates, and English toll collectors? Now, Sir, if you are so intensely anxious for the honour of your country as you express yourself to be, pray abandon at once and for ever this endless and silly cant about Rebecca and the *Chartists*. You must be aware that disturbances almost equally serious take place *annually* in some parts of England. Have you forgotten the British Riots, or has the reign of *swing* been obliterated from your memory?

(Revd Evan Jones, (Ieuan Gwynedd), *A Vindication of the Educational and Moral Condition of Wales*, 1848, p.9.)

C.15   In some instances the powerful influences of religion have been shamefully perverted . . . the colliers who signed the contract and returned to work have been solemnly excommunicated by the ministers of their several congregations. But ignorant men are most easily led by those who are only a shade less ignorant than themselves.

(*Cardiff and Merthyr Guardian*, 23 February 1850.)

Letter from Revd Thomas Price: 'It is well known in the neighbourhood and especially among the men, that I had previous to them leaving the pits, and since then up to the present time, endeavoured in every possible way to induce the men to go to work. The terms offered are not what I could have wished; still I firmly believed from the first that it would be better for the men to accept them and give them a fair trial.'

(*Cardiff and Merthyr Guardian*, 23 February and 2 March 1850.)

C.16   The Gospel rule for the regulation of the practical conduct of believers is clearly defined and rigid, demanding a stern *Nonconformity* to the principles, practices, and aims of the worldlings and godless. A Christian is one who has been 'called out of the world'. He is to live in the world where labour, provision and recreation are necessary conditions, but he is no longer of it. There is to be a sacred visible separateness or distinction between him, and those who are of it, though sometimes the nature and character of their toils and pursuits and pleasures may be identical. The followers of Christ are to be to men noble examples of self-denying abstinence from all excesses in business and pleasure, in eating and drinking and in dressing; moderate and reserved in all things pertaining merely to this life, that they may give proof of their heavenly citizenship.

(*Circular Letter of the Glamorgan and Carmarthenshire English Baptist Association*, 1875, pp.5–6.)

C.17   I should say the majority of our population is decidedly religious; but a small proportion only belongs to the Church of England, the remainder is in the government of the Dissenters, the *Independents*, who are the most important sect in this district. Their chapel is supported by the contribution of its members, and a large and well attended Sunday-school is connected with it. The *Baptists*, who command a large congregation, together with a Sunday-school. The Welsh *Calvinistic Methodists*, with their Sunday-school. I believe this sect will not admit any one as a member who belongs to any secret society. To this sect is to be attributed the growth of teetotalism in this place, 500 being about the number on the books of this society. The *Wesleyans* also are not numerous but highly respectable; and these comprehend the religious community here. They exclude political subjects entirely from their meetings, and in the 'break-outs' they are said to have exercised a somewhat beneficial influence over their respective congregations.

(*Report of the Royal Commission on Children's Employment (Mines)*, 1842, Vol.xvii, p.509. Evidence of J.C. Woolridge, cashier to the *Plymouth Works*, Merthyr.)

C.18   The Revd Griffith Ellis: 'The individual must not be sacrificed on the altar of society . . . Much of the poverty of our land is due to the habits of the people . . . If only our people would spend their earnings wisely, the problem of the unemployed would be to a great extent solved.'

(Presbyterian Church of Wales, *Report on Conference of English Churches*, 1895, p.33.)

C.19   Have the chapels been well attended since the works have been stopped? Yes, crowded. The preachers have alluded every Sunday to the unfortunate condition of the families, and have advised patience and resignation, and have been most attentively listened to. I am sure it is only a sense of religion that has kept them quiet. Ten years ago, under circumstances something similar, they were very outrageous, and would not allow those who had work to go to it; there is nothing of the kind now.

They, you say, are most of them ignorant, if they had education given them, as well as religion preached to them, they would still be peaceable and patient? Yes: still more so. Those who can read and write, I think, are the best amongst them. Education will never make men worse, but will surely improve their minds and dispositions, of that I am certain from long experience.

(*Report of the Royal Commission on Children's Employment (Mines)*, 1842, vol.xvii, p.415. Evidence of James Jones, Underground Agent, Ruabon.)

C.20 We as a company (Tredegar Iron Company) shall do our best to find employment for the people and help them to support themselves, their families and their religion . . . I take a great interest in the cause of temperance and I would suggest that you form a temperance society in connection with your chapel. Depend upon it, temperance will do a vast deal of good to the cause of religion.

(On the opening of the new Congregational (*Independent*) Chapel at Tredegar. *Merthyr Express*, 11 December 1875.)

C.21 In Wales the *Sunday Schools* are an institution of a peculiar character . . . They are composed of the congregations of the different places of worship which meet on Sundays, not only for worship, but also for the instruction of the young, and for a systematic discussion of religious topics, which goes on concurrently with the instruction. The adult classes choose one of their number as a teacher, or rather as a sort of leader of the discussion. The text book invariably is the Scriptures, each book being generally gone through chapter by chapter. The verses are read in succession by each member of the class and as each reader concludes, questions, if the passage suggests any, on the meaning, are addressed either by the teacher to the reader, or as frequently put by some member of the class to the other members. When the views of the class have been given, the teacher sums up the various opinions, and gives his own conclusions, with the reasons on which they are founded. The juvenile classes are principally occupied in learning to read, and in learning by heart passages of Scripture, hymns and other compositions of a religious character.

(*Reports of the Assistant Commissioners appointed to inquire into the State of Popular Education in England*, 1861, Vol.I, p.52.)

Capel Pembroke Terrace, Calvinistic Methodist church, Cardiff. Built in 1877.

C.22   It is this which accounts for the fact that such a large number of the common people in Wales are so much at home in the Holy Scriptures, and so well versed in theological knowledge. We do not mean to assert that all the Welsh people are thus, or even the greater part of them, but we do believe we are right in saying that it is so in the case of a larger proportion of the working classes than in any other part of the kingdom. Some time ago we passed three working men, we believe they were colliers, sitting together on a heap of stones by the roadside, and earnestly discussing the question 'How to reconcile the sovereignty of God with the responsibility of man'. It struck us at the time that people of that class do not usually discuss such subjects anywhere out of Wales. Perhaps we were mistaken; but we are certain that they would not have done it and would not have been able to do it, in Wales, if it had not been for its peculiar system of conducting the Sabbath School.

    (Revd D. Evans, *The Sunday Schools of Wales*, 1884, p.225.)

C.23   I have been here eleven years. Almost all the miners used to be drunkards and Sabbath-breakers. They would come to their work on Monday with bruised faces and black eyes. The change is beyond anything I ever knew. I saw great revivals in Cornwall but none to compare with the present awakening in these parts. They work here in companies of 4, 8, 12 and 20. There is no company without its prayer meeting underground before commencing work. They sing beautifully. On Saturday they gather together underground to render thanks for the mercies of the week. There is scarcely a house without its family altar.

    (J. J. Morgan, *The '59 Revival in Wales*, 1906, p.22.)

C.24   It was a rough lesson, and he trusted the lesson would not escape them. The worst times he remembered at Aberdare were religiously speaking the best times the workmen ever had. He turned the tide of his prosperity not into the good of his soul, but into the ruin of his soul and his body. The good times God gave him became the devil's own time; he it was who reaped a good harvest from them. Ah! Who does not remember when wages poured into the workman's lap like a stream flowing from the horn of plenty, the drinking, the debauchery, the spending there was . . . it is only by tethering us with affliction and trials that He prevents us from straying.

(*Cardiff and Merthyr Guardian*, 25 May 1850.)

C.25   At that time that awful pestilence the cholera was making terrible ravages throughout the manufacturing districts of Glamorgan and Monmouth. On the previous day Mr Rees, on his way to Beaufort, met many funerals, and saw scores of coffins carried through the streets of Merthyr Tydfil and other places, so that his own feelings as well as those of his hearers were unusually solemn. He was preaching the last of three at the ten o'clock service, on the second day of the association, with from ten to fifteen thousand people standing on the field before him. His text was that solemn sentence in Matt.xxiii.33, 'How can ye escape the damnation of hell?' After delivering with great power and feeling, for over half an hour many striking thoughts on the dangerous condition of impenitent sinners, the expression of his countenance and his voice suddenly changes, and then he shouted out with almost supernatural power and effect, 'IT IS POSSIBLE TO ESCAPE NOW.' Then he repeated the same words in a louder tone, and the third time in a still louder shout, until the whole of the vast multitude had lost all control over their feelings. Hundreds shouted for joy, and thousands cried out in agony for mercy. Such was David Rees as a preacher.

(Revd Thomas Rees, *The History of Protestant Nonconformity in Wales*, 1884, pp.474–5.)

C.26   Although many of the *Methodists* of this town have their roots in Blaenanerch, for their ancestors largely emigrated from South Cardiganshire, yet at that time there were not many here who had settled down from that district, for he (Owen Enos) found some difficulty in finding lodgings; not because of the housing problems of to-day so much, but he created a problem of his own by insisting on permission to conduct family worship twice a day, morning and evening. He had been accustomed to that fine old practice in the country, and religion to him was not a matter of latitude and longitude. He was very keen on removing the religious atmosphere of Cardiganshire to the benighted hills of Monmouthshire.

(Evan Price, *The History of Penuel Calvinistic Methodist Church, Ebbw Vale*, 1925, p.22.)

C.27   The *Nonconformist* bodies in Wales, especially the *Calvinistic Methodists* were composed at first almost wholly of working men. The great religious awakening began in the lower strata of society. The aristocracy of blood or money has never, as a class, been religious in any country — 'not many mighty, not many noble are called'. Now we are in danger of becoming too respectable. Not long ago, a very large number of our deacons were labourers — not workmen in factories and quarries merely, but farm labourers. That generation has almost all died out, and very few, if any, churches would now ever dream of electing a son of toil to be a deacon . . . The modern deacon is much more intelligent than some of his predecessors but perhaps he is less spiritual. The labourers were the representatives of a most important class, they were a bond of sympathy between the masses and the office bearers; and churches where working men were put in positions of trust had, and have, a claim and a hold on the working classes. They now look askance at the present diaconate of farmers and tradespeople as 'great folk in big pew'. One secret of influence of the Salvation Army is that men like themselves can rise in the ranks and are clothed with some authority.

(*Welsh Weekly*, 15 January 1892.)

C.28   We believe that God's will is to be done on earth in the polling booth and in Parliament as well as at the prayer-meeting, in the county council as well as in the missionary committee, on school boards, as well as in churches; that human life, in all its relations and interests, belongs to Christ.

(Revd James Owen, *The Free Churches and the People*, c.1890, p.29.)

C.29   Material conditions improved throughout the country and some felt this was partly due to religious influence, as at Wrexham. Following the opening up of new industries in any locality came the Shopkeepers and kindred groups serving the needs of the new communities. While the coalowners were not always active in religious activities, this middle group featured strongly in many types of religious organizations being frequently observed as secretaries and treasurers in the diaconate.

(Report, Evidence and Indexes of the Royal Commission appointed to inquire into the Church and other Religious Bodies in Wales, 1910, Vol.III, p.15.)

C.30   They are better dressed, better mannered, better cultured and better paid than the last generation of ministers and gradually they are placing the spiritual work of their fathers and the half-farming, half-preaching work of the grandfathers, on a higher social level.

(Red Dragon, vi, 1884, p.147.)

C.31   Chapel-building deserves particular notice. Most of the chapels built fifty and sixty years ago, with very rare exceptions, exhibited no architectural taste whatever. They were plain, unsightly buildings, more like barns or warehouses than places of worship. The comparative smallness and poverty of the congregations partly accounted for this; and also it was no easy matter to persuade the descendants of people who had been compelled for generations to worship God in caves, barns, and obscure cottages, that neat and costly places of worship were necessary and becoming. The least architectural ornament — pews instead of bare benches, and even brass chandeliers instead of clumsy iron candlesticks, the workmanship of the village blacksmith — were regarded by many as sinful innovations and signs of pride, unbecoming the humble worshippers of God. Those good people never called to mind the fact that the plan of the first place of worship erected on this earth came direct from heaven, and that the structure constructed in accordance to it was a very costly one. Those generations of mistaken Christians have passed away, and have been succeeded by a generation of more expanded ideas and a greater sense of propriety. There is now hardly any district in the Principality without a chapel or chapels which are ornaments to the locality. The old buildings are almost everywhere replaced by larger and superior structures, and hundreds of new chapels have also been lately erected where there were none before. In the Rhondda Valley, Glamorganshire, thirty years ago, there were only three small Dissenting places of worship; but now the number is seventy-one, and some of these are large enough to seat a thousand or twelve hundred people . . . The amount laid out by the *Nonconformists* of Wales within the last twenty-five years, in the rebuilding or renovation of old chapels and the erection of new ones, exceeds a million and a half. Congregations of farmers generally manage to pay for their new chapels on the day of opening, or soon after, but congregations of working men in the colliery and manufacturing districts take ten or fifteen years to do it.

(Revd Thomas Rees, *The History of Protestant Nonconformity in Wales*, 1884, pp.454–5.)

C.32 The character of the Welshman is rapidly becoming deteriorated. This is not the place to advance reasons for this assertion; nevertheless and not withstanding the able letters of the member for Merthyr (*Henry Richard*). It is a fact that will never be disproved that, wherever the Welsh give way to English teaching and become absorbed in the transactions of commerce, their minds attain an abnormal condition most detrimental to the encouragement of true religion. The result is, therefore, a compromise between religion and gold, between God and mammon, between respectability and meanness, in which the predominating factor is always that which furnishes the greatest amount of self-satisfaction.

(Anon., *Calvinistic Methodism in Wales: Its Present Position and Future Prospects*, 1870, p.34.)

C.33 With regard to the assertion 'that a great deal of time is expended upon instruction in the mother tongue of the people' there seems to be much misapprehension on the subject. If it be meant that 'instruction in the mother tongue of the people' is given with the exclusive view of perpetuating the Welsh language, then we maintain that the charge is utterly untrue, except in a very few instances. It is certain that Welsh children are now taught to read English in the day schools, and to understand that language for ordinary conversation; still Welsh is the great medium of communication, as yet, with the bulk of the population. And this is pre-eminently the channel of religious instruction, whether through the pulpit, the press, or the *Sunday School*. It is evident, therefore, that whatever time is devoted to the study of the language, is not for the sake of perpetuating it, but in order the better to profit spiritually thereby. The only time expended with the language exclusively as such, in addition to the mere mechanical labour of learning to read it, is that occupied with the explanation of the obsolete and unusual expressions of the Welsh Bible, which is indeed a peculiarity belonging to every language.

(Revd D. Evans, *The Sunday Schools of Wales*, 1884, p.355.)

C.34 If we wish to increase numbers as regards attendance upon public worship, much remains to be done; the gulf must be narrowed between the teachers and leaders of religion and the people; more of the spirit of Christianity must be shown; we must learn to come down from our lofty heights and exhibit more of the essence of that religion taught by the best and greatest of teachers, and one that has shown to the world the best mode of elevating each other.

(*Merthyr Express*, 31 December 1881.)

C.35 We hear discourses, sermons and even prayers on behalf of the poor and needy, but their text is 'Do as I tell you not as I do', for who are the deacons etc. of our churches, but shipowners, builders, shopkeepers, lawyers, etc., who can out of their surplus well afford to contribute liberally to the Church collection, at the same time screwing the wages of their poor workmen down to a minimum. The poor may remain in the back seat for a lifetime, without any of the big nobs pretending to know them for fear of defilement.

(*South Wales Daily News*, 26 August 1892.)

C.36   Both Churchmen and *Nonconformists* agree that Wales has now entered upon a profound intellectual and religious revolution on account of the vast and sudden increase of all kinds of educational opportunities now going on, and the recent rapid and resistless advance of English speech, literature and modes of thought. The most marked feature of Welsh religion in the past used to be a glowing fervour of Christian experience, with a practical outcome in morality, but with the emotional side distinctly prominent. This fervour of our fathers — whose loss a Welshman cannot mention without a passing sigh of regret — is generally acknowledged now to be a thing of the past among persons under middle age in Wales, and its place yet remains to be filled by a more intellectual and more complex — let us only hope it may be as true a form of the old — but ever new, spiritual life.

(Bishop of St Asaph quoted in *South Wales Daily News*, 7 October 1891.)

Debating the Evidence

In Dr Christopher Turner's essay *Nonconformity* in the nineteenth century becomes the central focus of attention. Dr Turner's sources are similar to those used in other essays in this volume. In dealing with the strength and attitudes of *Nonconformity* in nineteenth-century Wales, to what extent is the historian's interpretation shaped by the availability of sources? To the masses of people who embraced *Nonconformity*, was the appeal its system of belief and worship or its social and political context? Or was it a mixture of these things? Institutions like the *Nonconformist* denominations inevitably generated records as part of their dynamic existence and fortunately many have survived. Individuals — particularly the 'ordinary' chapelgoer — neither create nor leave behind personal material relating to their religious belief to anything like the same extent. The fragmentary nature of this evidence creates a historical distortion. The availability of mostly organizational material stressing the broader interests and activities of religious groups militates against understanding *Nonconformity* in terms of personal belief and worship. To what extent can we confidently assert that the views of *Nonconformist* denominational organizations, *Nonconformist* periodicals and the leaders of *Nonconformity* (lay and clerical) reflect the ideology and attitudes of *Nonconformists* as a whole? As ever in the study of great social movements (political and economic as well as religious) the historian must be careful not to represent the views of the organization (with its inevitable subjectivity) as being the same as, or representative of, the views of the individual. This, then, is not just a problem of approach by the historian — it is a problem of historical evidence. It is also important in assessing the impact of any great movement, such as *Nonconformity* in nineteenth-century Wales, for the historian to move away from internal evidence generated by the movement itself to external views, such as the counter-polemical (evidence emanating from the *Established Church*, for example).

Source C.1
There is elsewhere substantial reference to *Henry Richard*. Given this information, what do you see as being the strengths and weaknesses of the source?

Source C.2
What is meant by the term 'sittings' in this source and how does Dr Turner use such information to draw conclusions about the strength of *Nonconformity* in Wales? What evidence is there as to the relative strengths of the different *Nonconformist* denominations?

Source C.3
What kind of source is this? To what extent does the evidence on the extent of religious worship in Wales in C.2 contradict claims made by the author of this source?

Source C.4
Taking into account the basis on which Dr Turner has constructed this graph, what do you feel about its reliability as historical evidence?

Source C.5
As a source of information on the religious revival of 1859 in Wales what questions might you ask about the reliability of the evidence in this source?

Source C.6
Why do you think that historians find difficulty in locating evidence as to the scale of membership of religious bodies in nineteenth-century Wales? What might be the possible weaknesses of the evidence in this source?

Source C.7
In the light of Dr Turner's comments in his essay and the points made in 'Debating the Evidence' for Section E, assess the strengths and weaknesses of this source.

Source C.8
This extract is from a well-known series of anonymous reports on Wales which appeared in the newspaper, *The Morning Chronicle*, in 1851. What does it tell us about *The Morning Chronicle* and its readers?

Source C.9
What does the author have to say on the reasons for the strength of *Nonconformity* in Wales?

Source C.10
The strength of Welsh *Nonconformity* is accounted for in a different way in this extract. How does this differ from the reasons given in Sources C.8 and C.9? How reliable do you think this evidence is?

Source C.11
In 1824 the Combination Laws, which had made trade unions illegal, were repealed by Parliament. Bearing this in mind what do you make of the third declaration in this source? What questions would you need to ask about the reliability of this source as to the attitude of *Nonconformity* as a whole to trade *unionism*?

Source C.12
What does the author mean by his description of *Calvinistic Methodists* in the Newport area as being 'proper and Christian-like'?

Source C.13
How might the evidence here support an interpretation of the role of *Nonconformity* in nineteenth-century Wales as being that of 'social control'?

Source C.14
Considering the evidence discussed in Sections D and E of this volume, what assessment do you make of the evidence in this source?

Source C.15
What new light is thrown on the attitude of *Nonconformity* to trade *unionism*? In particular, consider the question of possible differences in attitude within *Nonconformity*.

Source C.16
What does this source suggest are the reasons why ordinary *Nonconformists* may have been influenced not to participate in trade union movements?

Source C.17
What questions might you ask about the reliability of this information? What other types of source might enable you to check the claims made here?

Source C.18
Is there anything here which contradicts information in C.17?

Source C.19
What are the strengths and weaknesses of this source?

Source C.20
What interpretation as to the role of religion in nineteenth-century Wales might be made from this information?

Source C.21
How reliable is this source in providing information on the *Sunday School* movement in Wales? How far is this complemented or contradicted in Source C.22?

Source C.23

What questions are necessary before assessing the reliability of this source as to the effects of the 1859 Religious Revival in Wales? What are the strengths of the testimony offered here?

Source C.24

What is the argument made here about the appeal of religion for the masses? Compare the information offered here and in C.19 on the lifestyle of working people.

Source C.25

Why, according to this information, did *Nonconformity* make more impact at some times than others? Do you accept this analysis?

Source C.26

Why would it be important to find out how this source was created in assessing its reliability? How might the evidence here be seen to contradict an argument made in Source C.14?

Source C.27

What reasons are given here for the decline of *Nonconformist* influence in Wales by the end of the nineteenth century?

Source C.28

On the question of the changing attitudes of *Nonconformity* in nineteenth-century Wales, compare evidence here with that in Sources C.16 and C.27.

Source C.29

How is the evidence here used to associate the growth of small business in Wales with the rise of *Nonconformity*? What other sources might provide evidence on this question?

Source C.30

On the question of changes in the background and experience of *Nonconformist* Ministers, compare the evidence here with that in Source C.8.

Source C.31

What reasons does the author of this source suggest for changes in the style of chapel building in nineteenth-century Wales? What type of source is this? How reliable is it?

Source C.32
What do you consider to be the strengths and weaknesses of this source in considering reasons for the decline in *Nonconformist* influence? Compare the evidence here with that in Source C.29.

Source C.33
What argument is put forward here about the relationship between the Welsh language and *Nonconformity*? Compare the evidence here with that in Source C.3.

Source C.34
What criticism of *Nonconformist* leaders is being made here? What questions would you need to ask about this source in assessing its reliability as evidence to support Dr Turner's point on working-class criticism of *Nonconformity*?

Source C.35
Compare the evidence here to that in Source C.27.

Source C.36
Consider the strengths and weaknesses of this evidence for Dr Turner's claim that immigration into Wales in the late nineteenth century weakened the influence of *Nonconformity*.

Discussion

Much of Dr Turner's evidence for the strength and influence of *Nonconformity* in nineteenth-century Wales is derived from within the movement itself. This is not to deny its validity or usefulness. However, when looking at the reasons for the strength of *Nonconformity* (for example, Sources C.9 and C.22) this must lead us to treat such sources with caution as well as respect. The evidence of an 'outsider', the Church of England vicar, the Revd John Griffith (Source C.10), is interesting in this respect. Not only does he provide a telling (unintentional?)

indication of the strength of *Nonconformity*, but also in discussing the reasons for this he reminds us that we have to consider negative as well as positive causes. Other sources (such as C.7, C.8 and C.21) appear to be from 'outside' observers of *Nonconformity* and supportive evidence for its strength and influence. This does not mean that the independence and reliability of such sources must not be challenged. Similarly Dr Turner's purpose here, which is to show the strength, influence and decline of *Nonconformity* in nineteenth-century Wales, needs to be set in the context of the judgement of other historians, including others in this volume. Some historians would point out, for example, that with all its flaws the *Religious Census of 1851* (Source C.2) demonstrates both the strength of *Nonconformity* and its weakness in that perhaps as many as half of the people of Wales attended no place of worship on 'Census Sunday'. As Dr David Jones reminds us in Section E there was 'another world' in the iron towns and colliery communities of south Wales where the pub, the *friendly society*, violence and crime were so prevalent. Evidence from within *Nonconformity* itself admits something of this in acknowledging the importance of revivals (Sources C.5, C.23). The historian of religion, as well as the historian of society, misses many crucial connections if he ignores religiosity or irreligiosity.

The Rebecca Riots

DAVID HOWELL

The Rebecca riots were the product of a dire poverty gripping
the farming community of south-west Wales during the late
1830s and the early 1840s. While the harvests of 1837 and 1838
were poor the country over, the three seasons from 1839 to 1841
in south-west Wales were atrocious, the wet and deficient
harvests rendering it incumbent on farmers to buy corn at
famine prices for their own use, thereby further eroding what
little capital they possessed. Nevertheless, sheep prices between
1839 and 1842 and butter prices between 1837 and 1841 were
high, and the low cattle prices of 1839 and 1840 also recovered
remarkably in 1841, so that a general fall in all prices occurred
only in 1842 and 1843. This general fall largely accounted for
the riots. Despite an early isolated outburst in 1839, the riots
really commenced in the winter of 1842 and continued
throughout 1843. Cattle prices slumped in south-west Wales in
1842, and the blame for this was directed at *Peel*'s tariff measures
of that year which eased the importation of foreign cattle and
meat. Butter and fat pig prices also fell in 1842. The harvest of
that year was the best seen in Wales for many years and this,
together with the diminution in demand from the Glamorgan
ironworks whose trade had slumped in autumn 1841, led to
corn prices falling steeply. Nor did the good corn harvest of
1842 much benefit livestock farmers though introducing
cheaper feed costs, for in 1843 the slump in the Glamorgan iron
trade, together with the new tariff, also meant that prices for
butter, cheese, pigs, store sheep, horses and lean cattle, upon
which the Welsh pastoral farmer primarily depended, were

D. 1   adversely affected (D. 1). Arguably, the combined effects of the demand for food from the iron centres eastwards and of the tariff were the crucial factors in precipitating the riots.

Faced with this drastic fall in income the farmers found no relief coming their way in the form of a reduction in their outgoings — rents, *tithes, poor rates*, county rates and *turnpike tolls*. On the contrary, these either remained constant (as their farm rents) or were actually increasing, as were their tolls, *tithes*, county rates and *poor rates*. In this situation they rightly saw themselves as the victims of 'tyranny and oppression' and in a spirit of recklessness, discontent and desperation they took the law into their own hands to rid themselves of unbearable burdens.

It was the *toll-gates* they first attacked, and there is no mistaking their loathing for the harshness of the *toll-gate* system. This 'oppression' set in from the late 1830s, when a group of English toll-renters, prominent amongst whom was the reviled Thomas Bullin, took over the trusts of the region and in return for paying higher rents for the gates made the mode of collection of tolls far more exacting. The worst grievance of the farmers was the big increase of side-bars (simple forms of *toll-gates*) on by-roads which were erected to catch any traffic, especially the all-important lime carts, which had skilfully joined and left the turnpike roads via side lanes to avoid the gates. These side-bars were hated as very 'catching' and a trick, and it was indeed the case that the discriminating Rebecca would sometimes attack only the side-bars and leave the 'legal'

D. 2   gates on the main roads intact (D. 2). *Toll-gates* were, however, but one among several grievances, and they were doubtless in large measure singled out for attack because they were tangible objects for farmers to lay their hands on and they were less easy to defend than were *union houses*. Arguably, the *Poor Law* was as much detested as turnpike gates, but farmers were powerless to attack *union houses* owing to their being garrisoned by troops. Arguably, too, rent and *tithe* were just as oppressive as tolls and affected more people, but it would have been extremely difficult to enlist a wide geographical area in a crusade against either. On the other hand, it would be unwise to play down overmuch the irksomeness of tolls *vis-à-vis* other burdens, for they saw the farmer's hand in his pocket constantly in the course of just one journey and so constituted an ever-present irritant. Indeed, we dare not underestimate the importance of tolls in seeking to explain Rebecca, for purely it was the erection of the many side-bars in this particular area to catch the elusive lime carts, together with the dependence of the farmers of south-west Wales, more so than those elsewhere in the Principality apart from the Vale of Glamorgan, upon the consumer market of the iron centres eastwards, which must largely explain why Rebecca was essentially a south-west Wales phenomenon.

Rebecca, it will be apparent, was also concerned at the high rents paid by farmers to their landlords and it is likely that had the latter made timely reductions the riots would not have occurred. By mid-July 1843 protest in the form of threatening letters was spreading from tolls to rents. Landlords were warned to make reductions. The summer of 1843 also saw large meetings being held demanding that rents should be lowered by at least a third (D.3) and in mid-September Rebecca was urging farmers in the parish of Penboyr and those parishes adjacent to petition their landlords, significantly in concert, to reduce their rents. For all the petitioning and threats of incendiarism and personal injury to landlords (D.4), agents and bailiffs, no great achievements were won in the face of farmers' competition for holdings and landlords' caprice. From late August onwards farmers were calling for regulation of rents by some form of independent assessment, thereby foreshadowing the late-century clamour for a land court in Wales to establish fair rents and fixity of tenure.

D.3

D.4

The furore over rents was justified, for apart from a number of commendable exceptions, most landlords failed to help their tenants. Rents were higher within Wales as a whole than in England. Many rents, indeed, under the system of leases for lives still common, remained at the level they had been charged in favourable years. For those farms coming up for re-letting, landlords were enabled to maintain the high level of previous rents because of the desperate demand for holdings arising from the anxiety of local inhabitants to rent a farm in their native area and from the fast growth in population. The situation was exacerbated by the common (though not general) practice of letting land to the highest bidder by tender. Landlords and tenants were both to blame (though the landlords more so) for this disgraceful system which resulted in exorbitant rents.

The working of the *Tithe Commutation Act* of 1836 was claimed by the Rebecca *Commissioners* inquiring into the riots to be second only to the turnpike system as a cause of discontent. Such opposition to *tithe commutation* was unique to south Wales, for elsewhere in Britain the business of commutation proceeded fairly smoothly. Circumstances were different in south Wales, where the *tithe* rent charge was borne by the occupier whereas in English areas the burden after commutation was borne by the landlord who, by undertaking it, rendered the collection easy and was enabled to let his land free from *tithe*. Doubtless because of this landowners in south Wales were careless in attending to the process of commutation and so let their tenants suffer by allowing higher amounts to be fixed than would otherwise have been the case. The Act meant that *tithe* payment in south Wales was increased by 7 per cent and considerably more so for south-east Wales. Though the increase was real enough, farmers misunderstood the principles underlying commutation and wrongly blamed the Act for imposing on them an unfair and heavy increase in payment. The real hardship arising from the working of the new legislation was that the price of corn in 1843 was depressed, so that the average price of corn for seven years upon which the annual *tithe* rent-charge was based was higher than the current 1843 price. Unlike the situation under the old system, after commutation little annual variation in the amount of payment was possible, however unprofitable the season to the farmer, and payment was now exacted rapaciously. And, of crucial impact on the farmers' besieged state of mind, *tithe* had now to be paid in money when D.5 they were very short of cash (D.5). This grievance over the financial burden of *tithe*, when merged with other factors especially acute in Wales, such as the great extent to which *tithes* had passed into the hands of laymen and the fast growth of *Nonconformity*, meant that payment of *tithe* in 1843 was bitterly resented.

Complaints against *tithe* were voiced from June 1843. And, with many of the toll-bars having by the end of August been destroyed or abolished, from that time opposition to *tithes*, high rents and the *New Poor Law* began to take precedence in Rebecca's programme. From June onwards mock auctions of *tithe* collectors were held (D.6) and threatening letters sent (D.7); an (unsuccessful) attempt to injure seriously the detested *tithe* agent, John Edwards of Gelliwernen House near Llannon (Carmarthenshire), was made in the night of 22–23 August by a large crowd of Rebeccaites; from early August 1843 protests against the burden of *tithes*, among other complaints, were made at daytime public meetings; and, foreshadowing the *Tithe War* of the 1880s (though the *tithe* issue had by then become more politicized and infused with nationalistic fervour thereby explaining its greater fury), at the *tithe* pay-day at Llandeilo on 27 August 1843, most of the farmers refused to pay, having the previous day requested a reduction.

The *New Poor Law* of 1834 was also hated by the lower orders. What rendered the farmers so angry at the legislation was that they were faced with an extra financial burden precisely at a time of acute scarcity of money and this new aggravating circumstance glaringly contrasted in their experience with the hitherto lax practice of permitting a man pressed for money to pay his poor rate in kind (D.8). Furthermore, in the rural parishes the operation of the Law meant an increase in the amount of rates compared with the old system (D.9) (though it should be appreciated that even under the earlier system a big increase of rates would have occurred in the early 1840s owing to the depression in both the agricultural and iron-manu-facturing areas). Farmers, too, were upset at the harsh bastardy clauses of the Act, both on grounds of their inhumanity and, predictably, because of the extra cost incurred when they operated. Although within the workhouse paupers seem to have been treated kindly and conditions of cleanliness and food were good and superior to those which were to be had outside, nevertheless the labouring classes hated the *New Poor Law* — above all, because they contended that their poverty was being treated as a crime and that they were being locked up in the cruelly-run *union house* as a prison (D.9). Also, they resented the insolence of the relieving officers.

While many farmers wished to return to something like the

D.6
D.7

D.8

D.9

D.9

old system of granting poor relief, several, particularly the better informed, were strongly opposed to this, desiring instead an amendment to the Act. Protest against the *New Poor Law* took the form of threatening letters being sent to masters of union workhouses warning them to empty the premises of paupers (D.10). Although Carmarthen workhouse was ransacked on 19 June 1843, the desired widespread assault on the execrated workhouses was frustrated by their being heavily guarded. Protest was also voiced against the *New Poor Law* at public daytime meetings and in a long Rebecca song in Welsh. (Rebecca songs also voiced other grievances.)

D.10

Rebecca was also concerned with the inflammatory issue of landholding. No one else, Rebecca stipulated, was to take treacherously a farm vacated by another because of a too-high rent (D.11) and an attempt was made through Farmers' Unions (though perhaps there were very few of these) and Rebecca's 'emissaries' (D.12) to obtain fair rents. Rebecca also forbade covetous farmers from holding more than one farm (D.13). Threatening letters warned the recalcitrant, and destruction of premises and incendiarism were the punishment visited on those who persisted in transgressing Rebecca's laws (D.11, D.12, D.13). This was basically an attempt (partially successful) by Rebecca to establish fixity of tenure as was then being advocated in Ireland.

D.11

D.12
D.13

D.11
D.12
D.13

In all her doings Rebecca was concerned with righting injustice, and this led her to settle a whole variety of what she deemed to be public and private wrongs perpetrated in the community. She strove to invoke traditional justice and to restore lost 'rights' to the community. Fathers of illegitimate children were forced to accept responsibility for their offspring (D.14); weirs adjudged to be illegally obstructing rivers and so interfering with the supply of fish, were destroyed; gentry of one area (Llangendeirne, Carms.) were warned off from shooting game as it belonged to Rebecca (Rebecca on another occasion desired that farmers be allowed to take game on their respective farms); individual farmers were warned against hoarding corn in expectation of a higher price; and, as an example of a private wrong being punished precisely in *ceffyl pren* tradition (which is discussed in more detail later), a cottager

D.14

and his wife had their furniture destroyed because the latter had testified against a neighbour stealing tobacco.

The riots, unlike the *Captain Swing* labourers' revolt of 1830–31, were a farmers' revolt. Labourers did not pay high rents, constant tolls, *tithes* and *poor rates*; indeed, they benefited from the current low prices even if jobs were scarcer. Nevertheless the labouring classes looked favourably on Rebecca, and agricultural labourers and, in south-east Carmarthenshire, colliers, were involved as lesser actors in the drama. In a very real sense, Rebecca was a community revolt and saw herself as such. Some farm labourers joined for positive reasons: they had close social ties with their employers, who tenanted only small farms and like themselves lived a threadbare existence; they hated the *poor law*; they resented paying tolls for potatoes which by custom they were permitted to plant in the farmers' fields. Moreover, labourers and boys joined in for 'a lark'; again, it was the joke at making fools of the authorities and military that kept many of the rioters out of bed; and some labourers were present at the express demand of Rebecca to certain farmers to present themselves along with their servants. But towards the end of August 1843 Carmarthenshire and Cardiganshire labourers, claiming to have helped their employers to get their grievances redressed, began to hold their own meetings to complain against the paltry way the farmers treated them (D.15). So alarmed were the farmers by this ominous twist of events that by late September 1843 they were welcoming the presence of troops. From late July 1843 the centre of Rebeccaism was to be increasingly found in semi-industrialized south-east Carmarthenshire. Here colliers, depressed through falling wages and unemployment, supported the farmers in smashing gates. Clearly, they had no quarrel with the gates and were diametrically opposed to the farmers' interests in wanting a reduction in food prices. Certainly the payment they received was a strong inducement; they may also have reasoned that support for the farmers would oblige the latter to support them in turn. Thus in early August the colliers resolved that inasmuch as they had assisted the farmers to get rents and tolls reduced they should call on them to lower the price of their produce. A further rift was opening up in the Rebecca movement.

D.15

1843 drawing of the Rebecca riots as depicted in the Paris magazine *L'Illustration*. (*Source: Mary Evans Picture Library.*)

Rebecca was not in her origins motivated towards political
D.16   change (D.16). Yet there was a radical spirit informing the west-
Wales peasantry born of their *Nonconformity*. Detestation of
church rates and particularly of *tithe* was pronounced. The
leadership of *Nonconformity*, however, generally disapproved of
Rebecca because of her violence. But below the ranks of the
official leadership it is likely that the dissenting ministers
provided their hearers with scriptural justification for their
action, even if they did not actually incite them to violence, as
the correspondent of the (usually) scrupulously fair London
D.17   newspaper *The Times* insisted was the case (D.17). Although the
peasantry were aware of *Chartist* ideas (both from the press and
Chartist emissaries travelling the countryside) and Rebecca and
the Merthyr *Chartists* both in turn invited the other to join their
ranks, it seems (contrary to what some, particularly the landed
gentry, averred) that *Chartist* emissaries and their ideas did not
win much support among the Rebeccaite peasantry, perhaps
D.18   because they were English (D.18, D.19). Albeit, with the
D.19   replacement of rioting by mass meetings from late August 1843
Chartist ideas could be, and were, more easily propagated,
especially by Hugh Williams, the Carmarthen *Chartist*, and the
massed gatherings certainly approved a call for the dissolution
of the present (unsympathetic) parliament, the extension of the
franchise and the ballot. In its later stages the Rebecca
movement exhibited more than a tinge of political disaffection.
For all that, unbearable poverty not political discontent led to
the outbreak of Rebecca, a poverty poignantly mirrored in the
heart-rending circumstances of a farmer's wife tearfully selling
her wedding ring in July 1843 because the sale of corn had not
raised sufficient to cover her rates — a circumstance arguably as
pregnant with pathos as the celebrated enforced sale of a
Dissenter's Bible (Penbryn parish, Cardiganshire) who would
or could not pay his tithes.

While farmers (apart from certain of their number during the
later stages of the revolt) were not politically disaffected, their
oppressive burdens filled them with loathing for the magistrates
and landowners for failing to redress their grievances,
D.20   for refusing to give them what they called 'justice' (D.20).
This want of confidence that the magistrates would listen to

their grievances, adopt a conciliatory spirit and grant them justice by removing oppressive exactions, was, indeed, one of the main causes of the riots. Their haughty, overweening demeanour towards the peasantry — treating them 'like dogs' when they appeared before the bench — was sorely complained

D.21   of (D.21). Magistrates' ignorance of the law, their decisions being influenced by their political opinions, and the influence exerted over them by uneducated clerks who, besides, charged oppressive fees, meant the peasantry could not obtain proper justice. Much of the obloquy against the tyrannical and arbitrary conduct of the magistrates was justified, but some was unmerited: after all, it was they who were given the thankless job of putting into operation 'unfortunate' recent legislation which was ill-suited to Welsh social conditions, the new taxation involved pressing peculiarly hard on the impoverished Welsh peasantry; and, with their estates encumbered, they simply could not afford to reduce their rents by between a third and a half as was popularly demanded.

    Not a little of the fascination of the riots lies in the manner in which they were enacted — men dressed in women's clothing, often white gowns, and having their faces blackened or wearing masks (though sometimes only some would wear female clothing), attacking *toll-gates* at night to the accompaniment of much noise and, in the early stages, a mock trial before the work of destruction. Such traits of female dress, blacking, noise and mock trials were a direct offshoot of the local practice of *ceffyl*

D.22   *pren*, significantly on the increase in the late 1830s (D.22). *Ceffyl pren* ('the wooden horse') was a way of frightening and punishing someone who had offended against the community's values, such as by marital infidelity or informing against another. The *ceffyl pren* was mirrored in the noisy, masked festivals of other European countries, as in the 'rough music' of certain English areas, in the charivaris, scampanate, katzenmusic and cencerrada, all forming part of The Abbeys of Misrule, bands of men who would mock the misdemeanours of neighbours. The carnival right of criticism and mocking sometimes spilled over into real social protest across Europe, Britain and Ireland in the early modern period, when men wore women's clothing — in Wales we see it in the striking colliers of south Wales between 1830–32 and, of course, in the Rebecca riots. Ritual and festive inversion were being put to new uses.

In part, of course, the black face and female attire was a simple matter of disguise. But equally important, argues Natalie Davis,[1] were the various ways in which the female persona sanctioned resistance. 'On the one hand the disguise freed men from full responsibility for their deeds and perhaps too from fear of outrageous revenge upon their manhood. After all, it was mere women who were acting in this disorderly way. On the other hand, the males draw upon the sexual power and energy of the unruly woman and on her license (long assumed at carnival and games) to promote fertility, to defend the community interests and standards, and to tell the truth about unjust rule.' In similar vein, other historians such as Alun Howkins and Linda Merricks[2] point to how participation in the ritual of blacking and wearing women's clothes transforms those involved; blacking the face or wearing a mask was not just a matter of concealment. Indeed, the real element of concealment was against the self, for behind the ritual of mask, female garb and acting the 'pantomime' of resistance, respectable farmers (in Rebecca's case) could become transformed into the community's conscience and carry out acts of protest totally out of character with their respectable selves. This fascinating insight into the sexual symbolism and topsy-turvy play involved in transvestism and into the ritual of blacking, enrichens our understanding of the riots. We are left wondering whether resorting to turning one's coat inside out, occasionally adopted by Rebeccaites, was simply a matter of disguise.

From late August 1843 public protest meetings were replacing riots, partly because the farmers were drawing back from violence and partly because the presence of troops was inducing caution. But though fewer, the riots grew more violent. The terrifying activities of a gang of miscreants masquerading as Rebecca and operating from Five Roads, near

---

[1] Natalie Z. Davis, 'Women on Top: Symbolic Sexual Inversion and Political Disorder in Early Modern Europe' in B.A. Babcock (ed.), *The Reversible World: Symbolic Inversion in Art and Society*, Cornell University Press, 1978.

[2] Alun Howkins and Linda Merricks, ' 'Wee be black as Hell': ritual, disguise and rebellion', an unpublished paper, kindly made available by the authors.

Llanelli, led by the unsavoury Shoni Sguborfawr and his henchman, Dai'r Cantwr, by late September had turned respectable farmers of that area against Rebecca. Also, as shown, farmers of west Wales were worried during September by the strident tone of their labourers. Accordingly, by the end of the month the farmers themselves had brought Rebecca to a halt, only isolated instances occurring henceforth on the periphery of the region.

The name 'Rebecca', was taken from the scriptural reference to Rebecca in Genesis 24 : 60, and identified several Rebeccas in different areas, for the movement had no one master-mind and spread over the countryside by imitation. Though sometimes exaggerating her grievances (thus separation of husbands from wives and their families in workhouses happened less in practice than was claimed and, indeed, the workhouse test was not universally put into practice) and misconceiving the real situation, and sometimes needlessly violent, malicious and vengeful on her enemies (intimidation of fellow-farmers by 'Becca, however, is surely understandable given the nature of that society), Rebecca was a noble-minded movement on the part of a downtrodden peasantry to obtain 'justice', which their leaders so unfeelingly withheld. The riots have been rightly viewed as deriving basically from a fast-rising population overstretching the resources of a backward farming economy and proving too much for an outdated administrative machinery to cope with. In good years the farmers could struggle on, but under acute depression they folded. Matters were worsened by government legislation manifestly unsuited to Welsh conditions and which further harassed the peasantry. Trustees of turnpike roads, landlords, agents and bailiffs, magistrates, *tithe* owners and agents, *poor law* officials and, not to be downplayed, English toll-farmers like Bullin and English land-stewards, all incurred Rebecca's wrath. In her self-proclaimed 'journey of doing good to the Poor and distressed farmers' Rebecca gained real achievements. During the course of the movement itself, there were secured an amelioration of the *toll-gate* burden (nonetheless toll-houses destroyed in the riots had to be re-erected after the riots had ended) and certain modest rent reductions from some landlords at least. Later, a

Turnpike Act of July 1844 consolidated the trusts, county road boards taking over all the trusts in each shire. Tolls were simplified and made more uniform and the grievous toll on lime cut by half. Rebecca, moreover, was to furnish an inspiration for later Welsh rural protest.

Sources

Depressed Prices

D.1 I am told however that for two or three years before the last Harvest [1842] the crops had been unusually deficient, so that not only had they no surplus to dispose of, but in many instances were obliged to purchase for their own use.

    The Harvest of last year, however, was above on average; and this, combined with the diminution of demand in the iron districts of Glamorganshire, and the neighbourhood, has had the effect of throwing down prices in a ruinous proportion. Barley, which last year fetched 6s/ the Winchester bushel, realises 3s/6. Other corn has fallen almost in the same proportion. Cheese from 3 1/2d. and 4d. to 2d. Butter likewise. A large farmer at Newcastle Emlyn, who has ordinarily carried over 2 Cwt of butter per fortnight to Glamorganshire can scarcely now sell this same quantity at the reduced price, once a month. Horses are almost unsaleable — lean cattle, low — but, I think, not *so* low.

(William Day, from Carmarthen, to George Cornewall Lewis, 9 July 1843 — Public Record Office, Home Office papers, 45/1611.)

Toll-gates

D.2 [The farmers meeting at Llangendeirne (Carms.) on 1 August 1843 to discuss tolls of the Kidwelly Trust] say there is not a by-lane of any sort by which a cart can get to the lime-kilns which has not a bar or chain across it. They say if ever there is a lane by which one or two farmers can get to their farms, without paying toll, an application is immediately made to the trustees to grant a bar on the lane, which is always of course acceded to; that there is never a fair held in any of the villages or principal towns but the toll contractor surrounds the town by every approachable access to it with a cordon of toll-bars. Chains are fastened across the roads close to the town, and thus they catch every farmer who has cattle, or sheep, or horses, or carts to bring to the fair . . . In many of these lanes, by going a mile or two round, the farmers could escape toll. The lanes are kept in repair by the parishes, and are many of them quite as good as the high roads of the trusts . . . it is impossible for a farmer to stir two miles from home in any direction without having a bar or gate to pay toll at. This, with the fact that many of these roads are maintained by themselves, naturally has greatly exasperated them, and the toll bars and gates are continually being demolished.

(*The Times*, 4 August 1843: 'from our own reporter', Carmarthen, Tuesday, 1 August.)

Rents

D.3 They are not satisfied now with *tollgates*, but they hold large meetings frequently in the daytime and demand that rents shall be lowered by at least a third .. Our own tenants [of Middleton Hall estate, near Llandilo] have signed and sent to Mr Adams [the landlord] a petition demanding rather than requesting a return of not less than a third of their Rents — Many of these Rents are very low but generally they are shamefully high.

(Thomas Cooke, steward of Middleton Hall, to his mother in England, 24 August 1843 — in National Library of Wales MS. 21209C.)

D.4 Mynachlogddu June 19, 1843
William Peel Esq.,
Sheriff [of Carms.]
Taliaris

Sir, . . . in my journey of doing good to the Poor and distressed farmers I took notice of *you as one* who not careful enough of your Tenantry do by your oppressing and arbitrary power make them to languish under your hand. You know very well I dare say that every article the farmer has to sell is of a very low price in this county [Carms.] and you know too well that your rent is as high as ever therefore if you will not consider in time and at your next Rent day make a considerable allowance to your Tenantry I do hereby warn you in time to mind yourself for as sure as this letter will come to your hand I and my dutiful daughters from 5 to 10 hundred of us will visit your habitation at Taliaris in a few days and you will do well to prepare a secure place for your soul we will do well with your body your flesh we will give to the Glansevin [a Carms. estate] hounds and your bones we will burn with those of Sir James Williams [of Edwinsford] and Lewis Gilfach in Tophet [symbolic for the torments of Hell, or Hell itself] unless you and them will make more good to the poor farmer than you do. Down the rent and all will be good.

I remain your faithful

Servant Rebecca Do good

(A Rebecca threatening letter housed in Public Record Office, Home Office papers, 45.454.)

Tithe

D. 5 The Tithes have generally been taken in kind, and, odious as the system was, habit had rendered it tolerable. The farmer indeed lost the tenth part of his Crop, and was moreover exposed to annoyances in the harvesting of it — but that done there was an end of the question till the next year, and he had no further solicitude on the Subject. If the crop was abundant, the Parson carried off the larger quantity — if scanty, his proportion was reduced — not so, however, now — the Commutation is fixed — and alters slowly with every seventh year — the amount is to be paid with little annual variation, however unprofitable may be the season to the farmer — and is to be paid *in money*.

(W. Day, from Carmarthen, to George Cornewall Lewis, 9 July 1843, in Public Record Office, Home Office papers, 45/1611.)

D.6   A *tithe* Collector of ye name of Morgan living near Llangrannog
       was I am told sold in this way [i.e. by mock auction] a few nights
       ago. The purchase was declared as 'The Devil' and ye security
       was given in ye name of ye Clergyman of ye parish.

(Letter of Edward Crompton Lloyd Hall, a Liberal barrister and
heir to Cilgwyn estate [Cards.], to Sir James Graham, the Home
Secretary, 23 June 1843 in the Public Record Office, Home
Office papers, 45/454.)

D.7   Evidence before the Rebecca *Commissioners* of Revd Eleazar
       Evans, vicar of the parish of Llangrannog and Llandissilio-
       gogo (Cards.)

They request me [in a threatening letter of 'Becca', 5 August
1843] to send back the advance in *tithes* and the law expenses by
such a day, and that Becca and her daughters are sure to take
notice of me if I do not do so; that Becca had found a place for
my body, and they desired me to find a place for my soul, and
the place for my body was to be at the end of the National
Whore, that is at the end of the *Established Church*, that is the title
they give to it.

(*Minutes of Evidence before the Commissioners of Inquiry for South
Wales*, 1844, set up specifically to inquire into the riots.)

The New Poor Law
D.8   Many of the complaints upon the subject of the *Poor Law* are
       traceable to that cause, which is at the root of most of the 'Welsh
       grievances', the poverty of the people, and the difficulty of
       finding wherewithal to meet the continual demands of local
       taxation. Under the lax and irregular system which formerly
       prevailed in the rural districts, the Poor-rate was frequently paid
       in grain or in any other commodity more convenient at the time
       for the farmer to part with than money . . . In this instance again
       the enforcement of a definite pecuniary impost in lieu of the
       cheaper and more indulgent system of composition heretofore
       allowed has fallen with the weight of a new tax on the occupier
       of the land.

(*Report of the Commissioners of Inquiry for South Wales*, 1844.)

D.9 I [the Times reporter] had the question put to the meeting [of about 100 farmers at Conwil Elfed, Carms., on 16 August, 1843] — 'If the poor generally were satisfied with their treatment in the workhouse?'

The answer was, 'No; when they are sent to the workhouse the poor think they are going to be incarcerated there, the same as if any one of us were to be sent to prison.'

A farmer said, 'Under the old system we relieved and maintained our poor among ourselves. The former system [of outdoor relief as distinct from sending the able-bodied poor to the workhouse] was not nearly so costly . . .'

I had the question put, 'Is the *New Poor Law* as unpopular amongst the farmers and ratepayers generally as it is amongst the poor?' The answer was, 'Everyone is against it.'

I then had the question put to the meeting in Welch [sic] — 'If you had the power, would you wish to return to the old system of relieving the poor, in preference to the present?'

The answer was an immediate and unanimous shout, 'Yes, tomorrow, if we could.'

(*The Times*, 19 August 1843. 'From our own reporter', Conwil, 16 August.)

D.10 [Translation of original sent in Welsh]
Avenging of blood.
June 19 1843

As thy soul liveth and as we live if thou do not come out thou and the paupers that are under thy care before next Wednesday we are determined to destroy it wholly and woe be to thy body for we shall take care of thee that thou shalt not escape (!Beware!) joke we do not any more.

Rebecca
Miss Brown
[to] Mr Davies
Ye Master of ye
Union Workhouse
Newcastle Emlyn

(Public Record Office, Home Office papers, 45/454.)

REBECCA
AND HER
DAUGHTERS.

WELSHMEN,

You have sent me a letter commanding me to appear on WEDNESDAY night at BLAEN-NANT-LANE, armed and disguised. That your object is to obtain redress for some of the grievances with which you are oppressed is evident. But this is not the way to obtain such redress. I have been, as you know, labouring for years to gain you the rights of free men, and now that I begin to see the possibility of doing some good for you, you step in, and by your violence and folly hinder me in the good work; and instead of hastening the time when all your grievances will be at an end, your nonsensical extravagance gives an excuse to your oppressors for refusing to listen to your complaints; and the redress you seek is further off than ever. GET ONE GRIEVANCE REDRESSED AT A TIME. The Magistrates and Trustees of the Newcastle and Carmarthen Trust have appointed **Friday the 23d Instant to OVERHAUL THE GRIEVANCES CONNECTED WITH THAT TRUST.** I have been retained on the part of the Men of the Hundred of Upper Elvet to represent their interests at such Meeting. **Do you think I will neglect my duty? Do you think it is likely I should flinch from insisting on justice being done to the people? Or do you think that I am ignorant of the means of screwing it out from the Trustees, let them be as reluctant as they will?** They have not been accustomed to be brought authoritatively to account. Like young ones not broken, they must be treated at first both gently and firmly. Do you think any firmness is wanting in me? Why then will you do anything that will prevent my getting the bridle into their mouth?

Do you think I can countenance or join your riotous proceedings? I tell you No. And what is more, though I have fought, am fighting, and will continue to fight your battles, until I can obtain perfect justice and political regeneration for you and your children, I am and will always be the first man to keep the Queen's peace, and prevent anything like rioting or disturbance. Enough has been done already to convince the Government of the great and universal discontent which your grievances have caused among you. They have sent down soldiers to keep the peace. **I therefore entreat you not to meet together on Wednesday night.** I have written for the soldiers to come here and prevent your doing any mischief if you should. Why will you hinder me from fighting your battles in the only way in which we can be successful; and by your violence and absurdity, which can do no good, turn me from a friend to an enemy? Your conduct is childish and absurd, and not like men who have great objects to attain. Why will you exhibit folly when wisdom is required? **The penalty for pulling down a Turnpike House is TRANSPORTATION FOR LIFE.** What good can you get by running such a risk, when you may attain every thing you ought to have, in a peaceable and quiet manner, without running any danger whatever? I can only attribute it to your ignorance, which prevents you from being able to guide in its proper course the great and irresistible force which you possess. A hundredth part of your strength properly applied, will do more for you, and without risk, than a thousand times your power wasted in the absurdities you have lately indulged in. Be guided by me. Do what I tell you, and **you must be victorious in the end.** Go each one to your own homes on Wednesday night, peaceably and quietly. On Thursday morning, let each Parish choose two Delegates to come to me (as the Parishes in the Hundred of Upper Elvet have done,) to make me acquainted with your grievances, and then follow implicitly the advice I shall give them. If you do, peace and prosperity will be sure to return to you. If you do not, I shall leave you to enjoy the results of your ignorance and folly.

EDW. CR. LLOYD HALL.

Emlyn Cottage, Newcastle-Emlyn,
June 20th, 1843.

Appeal of the gentry to the followers of Rebecca. (*Source: Dyfed Archives, Carmarthen Record Office, Bryn Myrddin Collection.*)

Regulation of landholding

D.11   No farm which has been vacated is to be taken by another *or else*
        — these two last words close all their threats.

        (Thomas Cooke, Middleton Hall steward, to his mother, 24
        August 1843 — National Library of Wales MS. 21209C.)

D.12   The county of Carmarthen is being valued by the Emissaries of
        these miscreants, and any Farmer who pays more for his farm
        than their ideal standard will have the midnight incendiary to
        enlighten him of his error.

        (J. Lloyd Davies, Esq., of Alltyrodyn Mansion, Cards., 17 June
        1843 to Home Office, in Public Record Office, Home Office
        papers, 45/454.)

D.13   It is only within these few days that I received information of
        one incendiary fire that was completed, another that broke out
        and was extinguished almost immediately; and I am led to
        believe that those fires were in consequence of the parties who
        owned the property having a farm, and another portion of land
        which they held as well, and that the fire was supposed to be the
        visitation of Rebecca for that supposed offence. About a
        fortnight or three weeks ago, there was a threatening notice
        placed upon the door of a farmer in the neighbourhood of
        Whitland, . . . and his offence was supposed to be that of
        holding three farms, I think.

        (Evidence of Col. George Rice Trevor, Vice-Lieutenant of
        Carms., before Rebecca Commissioners, 7 November 1843, in
        *Minutes of Evidence before the Commissioners of Inquiry for South
        Wales*, 1844.)

Correction of public and private wrongs

D.14   In ye same parish [Llanfihangel-ar-arth] a gentleman farmer a
        Mr Bowen of Wernmackwyth . . . had a visit from 'Rebecca and
        her daughters' who brought with them a child which they told

him was an illegitimate of his own and on pain of having his premises fired, made him promise to take care of it in future.

(Letter of Edward Crompton Lloyd Hall to Sir James Graham, 24 August 1843, in the Public Record Office, Home Office papers, 45/454.)

Farm Labourers and the riots

D.15 I hear that they [farm labourers] are holding meetings every night on the hills in this county [Carms.] and Cardiganshire. They complain that the farmers pay them ill and treat them badly. They say to the farmers, 'We have heard your grievances and helped you to get them redressed; and now we will tell you ours'. I have heard of several meetings of this kind in which the labourers have pretty loudly grumbled at their treatment by the farmers, in being underpaid . . . The farmers are beginning to express much alarm at these proceedings.

(*The Times*, 5 September 1843: 'From our own reporter', Carmarthen, 30 August.)

Rebecca and Politics

D.16 It is a matter of great satisfaction to state our belief that the disturbances of the country, though so widely extended, were not connected with political causes, and that nothing like a general spirit of disaffection, or organised hostility to the laws, pervaded the community.

(*Report of the Commissioners of Inquiry for South Wales*, 1844, p.1.)

D.17 I was rather surprised to learn during my inquiries that the text I sent to you some time ago, the 24th chapter of Genesis, and 60th verse, on which the Rebeccaites are said to found their proceedings, has frequently been preached from in the *Baptist*, *Independent*, and Dissenting chapels, and that the preachers have advised the people of their outrageous proceedings. The *Wesleyan Methodist* preachers, on the contrary, have pursued an opposite course, and have urged the people not to break the law.

(*The Times*, 29 July 1843, reporting on 'the State of South Wales'.)

D.18   *Poor Rebecca!* . . . You are a *Chartist*! Why, you don't know the meaning of the word. A political incendiary! — Politics and you are perfect strangers — more's the pity and the worse for you.

   (*The Welshman*, editorial, 21 July 1843 — a radical newspaper.)

D.19   It seems the impression of several gentlemen and magistrates with whom I have conversed that many *Chartists* are prowling about the country and doing a great deal of mischief. Numbers of strangers are about who conduct themselves suspiciously. I much doubt, however, if such be the case, whether they meet with any success. It is difficult to stuff the head of a Welsh farmer, who speaks and reads only Welsh, with the political crotchets of *Chartism*.

   (*The Times*, 18 August 1843 — 'from our own reporter', Carmarthen, August 15.)

Justice and the Magistrates

D.20   I inquired, — 'You state your chief grievance to be that you cannot get redress for oppressive exactions. Now, if you could get what you call 'justice from the magistrates', would the present disturbances cease?'

   A farmer who spoke English answered — 'My opinion is, if we could only get justice, it would be perfectly unnecessary to have either soldiers or policemen . . . if proper means of redress were afforded there would be no disturbances in Wales. If the magistrates now would only take proper means to satisfy the country by doing simply justice they may take away the soldiers whenever they please.'

   (*The Times*, 19 August 1843, reporting a Rebecca meeting of 100 farmers at the Blue Bell Inn, Conwil Elfed (Carms.) on 16 August.)

D.21   That conduct of the magistrates at petty sessions is quite unbearable that we are treated like dogs we are told to hold our tongues or go out of the room, and the law that is dealt out to us is the law of the magistrate's clerk and not the law of the Queen, and the magistrates' clerks charge us what they please.

(National Library of Wales MS 14590E: Letter 18 (no date), but referring to a statement made at the Conwil Elfed meeting of Rebeccaites of 16 August 1843.)

D.22   *Ceffyl Pren and Rebecca*

And as *Turnpike tolls* are most extraordinarily heavy and ye gates placed upon ye most catching system throughout this country, they naturally endeavour to relieve themselves of that burden and there being a custom in this part of ye country called carrying 'Ceffil pren' . . . ye mode of getting rid of such a grievance by nocturnal violence is perfectly familiar to their minds.

(Edward Crompton Lloyd Hall to Sir James Graham, 15 June 1843, in Public Record Office, Home Office papers, 45/454.)

Debating the Evidence

David Howell's essay examines popular protest in rural Wales. He uses a wide range of evidence to try to reconstruct the secret nocturnal activities of the Rebecca Rioters in south-west Wales. He demonstrates, in particular, the way in which historians use evidence to deal with causation in history. Amongst the sources he uses for this is a remarkable series of reports which appeared in *The Times* newspaper. In this case we know a great deal about the author of the reports and his closeness to events he describes. Thomas Campbell Foster was a young reporter sent to west Wales to investigate the unusual events taking place there. He appears to have made exhaustive enquiries into the causes of unrest, to have won the confidence of the farmers who participated in and supported protest and, in his reports, to have faithfully and evocatively recorded social conditions in the area. Dr Howell also draws on official Government records, in particular those of the Home Office. Often such sources frustrate the historian who wishes to get behind bureaucratic reaction to seek the real causes of mass social protest. However, in this period before widespread policing, the

Home Secretary was empowered to despatch available police forces and the soldiery to areas menaced by social unrest. Thus he was liable to receive plaintive requests from 'responsible' citizens in such areas and it is this type of material which is particularly useful to Dr Howell.

Source D.1
George Cornewall Lewis was the Chairman of the *Poor Law Commissioners*, the body responsible for administering the *New Poor Law* of 1834. William Day was a Sussex farmer who became an Assistant *Poor Law Commissioner* and implemented many of the provisions of the *New Poor Law* in west Wales. What bearing has this information on the reliability of the evidence here?

Source D.2
What are the strengths and weaknesses of this report by Thomas Campbell Foster? What type of evidence might give us the views of members of the Turnpike Trusts on these questions?

Source D.3
In what way might the evidence in Source D.1 have a bearing on developments described in this source? Why do you think that, in view of his job, Thomas Cooke's evidence is particularly revealing?

Source D.4
What do you think is meant by the phrase 'not careful enough of your tenantry do by your oppressing and arbitrary power make them to languish under your hand'? What might the existence and the style of this letter tell you about the Rebecca movement?

Source D.5
Check the definition of the terms 'taken in kind' and 'commutation'. Why do you think that the payment of *tithes* in money was such a problem for farmers in west Wales?

Source D.6
What is the problem in understanding this source? Why might you question its reliability?

Source D.7
Why do you think the evidence here could be regarded as more reliable than that in D.5 and D.6? Does this source have any weaknesses?

Source D.8
What is meant by the passage 'a definite pecuniary impost in lieu of the cheaper and more indulgent system of composition heretofore allowed'?

Source D.9
Why do you think this source and D.2 might be said to be particularly strong evidence as to the causes of the Rebecca Riots? What other kinds of evidence might exist as to attitudes to the *New Poor Law* in west Wales?

Source D.10
Why does the anonymity of this source create a problem for historians?

Source D.11
Explain the point that Thomas Cooke is making here.

Source D.12
Given the brief details about J. Lloyd Davies, and the tenor of his evidence, how reliable do you think this source is?

Source D.13
What does this source reveal about the attitude of the Rebecca Rioters? What are the weaknesses of D.11, D.12 and D.13 as evidence for the attitudes of Rebecca's supporters over landholding?

Source D.14
What does this source tell us about Rebecca's stance on moral issues? What questions might you ask about the reliability of this evidence?

Source D.15
Do you think this report by Thomas Campbell Foster is as reliable as those in Sources D.2 and D.9? Why does Dr Howell see the evidence presented here as being important in the development of the Rebecca Riots?

Source D.16
What questions need to be asked about the reliability of this source?

Source D.17
What other types of evidence might be consulted to check the claims made here?

Source D.18
What is there about this source which might lead us to see it as particularly strong evidence of the lack of political motivation for the Rebecca Riots?

Source D.19
In what way does Source E.12 appear to contradict the evidence here?

Source D.20
Noting particularly the circumstances in which it originated, list the strengths and weaknesses of this source.

Source D.21
Which of the two sources dealing with this event do you see as being more reliable — D.20 or this one?

Source D.22
What point is made here about the links between Rebecca and *Ceffyl Pren*? Why might you regard this evidence as less reliable than D.20 and D.21?

Discussion

The main thrust of David Howell's essay is the deployment of evidence to demonstrate the wide range of discontents which contributed to the Rebecca disturbances. This provides a corrective to the over-simplistic interpretation which concentrates just on the grievances against Turnpike Trusts. These the author sees as a symbol of broader dissatisfaction. Thereby the complexity of causation in history is exhibited. At his best, Thomas Campbell Foster (D.2, D.9, D.20) makes clear the value of informed journalistic reportage as a means of gaining a direct insight into the views of Rebecca's followers. Apart from the anonymous Rebecca letters (D.4 and D.10) which provide problems precisely because of their anonymity, *The Times* reports are the only direct evidence we have of the views of Rebecca's followers. It could be argued that much of the other material is particularly difficult to handle either because it derives from those who suffered at the hands of Rebecca (not that this means it is not of value) or because it concerns events observed at some distance. This latter is true of the report of the Commission which enquired into the Rebecca Riots (D.7, D.8, D.13, D.16). Whilst the Commissioners toured west Wales extensively and invited evidence from all who wished to give it, only the local gentry and magistrates actually provided it. The letters and reports sent to the Home Office (D.1, D.5, D.6, D.12, D.14, D.22) suffer from a similar limitation. Their authors are trying to alert the Home Office and encourage intervention. The letters of Edward Crompton Lloyd Hall (D.6, D.14, D.22) are particularly problematic in this respect. He was a young barrister who had inherited the Cilgwyn Estate in Cardiganshire. He was, however, an ultra-radical in politics and greatly disliked by his fellow gentry whom he often attacked. Why, therefore, did he supply the Home Secretary with this detailed evidence on Rebecca? As most of it appears to rely on hearsay there is an additional query over the reliability of his evidence. Dr Howell reveals both the delicate balance which historians have to maintain in handling such evidence and the way in which, despite the difficulties, it allows us some insight into the complexities of such profound social dislocations as the Rebecca Riots.

Scotch Cattle and Chartism

DAVID J.V. JONES

The extent to which Britain was a class society during the period of the industrial revolution has long been a matter of debate amongst historians. By the 1840s there was a general acceptance that a working class had emerged, with its own values and ambitions. In a number of regions this class consciousness reached such an intensity that the authorities were seriously alarmed. The novelists of the time located this fear in the north-west of England, but ministers of the crown probably regarded the inhabitants of the Principality with the deepest suspicion. Wales was being transformed in these early decades, and the appearance of *combinations*, strikes and riots was a clear sign of the resulting tensions. In the 1820s there were claims that power in the south Wales coalfield was falling into the hands of the *Scotch Cattle*, an illegal terrorist organization, and in the following decade the same area witnessed two of the most daring attempts at revolution in modern British history. The Merthyr and Newport Risings were proof, if proof were needed, that beneath the apparently quiet surface of Welsh life,
E.1   dangerous forces were at work (E.1).
Until quite recently these popular movements were regarded with some disapproval by writers on modern Wales. From the days of *Henry Richard* in the mid-nineteenth century, there was a feeling that the excesses of the *Scotch Cattle* or the *Chartist*
E.19   miners were best forgotten (E.19). Only one, anonymous, person wrote an account of the former movement, and none of the leaders of the *Newport Rising* could be persuaded to recall the events of 4 November 1839. The memory of such class hostility did not suit the mid-Victorian mood of social improvement and

harmony. Nor did it relate to the growing preoccupation with radical *Nonconformity* and gradual constitutional change. With a few exceptions, historians in the twentieth century have also condemned the early expressions of class anger and violence. E.W. Evans (in *The Miners of South Wales*, Cardiff, 1961, p.51) claimed that the *Scotch Cattle* was a 'disreputable' movement of criminals and miners, whilst David Williams (*John Frost: A Study in Chartism*, Cardiff, 1939) was saddened by the futile violence of Welsh *Chartism*.

To make greater sense of both movements, it is necessary to appreciate the backgrounds from which they came. The south Wales coalfield, which was the scene of so many of the disturbances of the first half of the nineteenth century, was a frontier society. Prints of the period capture the reality of the monstrous black ironworks and the smoke-filled valleys. Up on the hillsides the 40,000 ironminers and colliers lived in their grey barracks, with their diseased and poverty-stricken families. Most of them were first-generation immigrants, who had travelled from the neighbouring counties, seeking wealth and freedom. Poverty was not a novel experience for these people, but the relationship between them and their employers was. The first great ironmasters in their mansions, and the non-resident coalowners, were unabashed capitalists who saw neither point nor profit in paternalism. Only the smallest amounts of money were expended on schools, churches and social welfare. Despite denials, social relationships in the area were always insensitive and sometimes brutal. H.S. Tremenheere, an education inspector sent down to the area after the *Newport Rising*, told the government that class hostility was the norm (E.2).

E.2

Another aspect of the social background which helps to explain the popular movements in the second quarter of the nineteenth century was the exceptional feeling of community solidarity. Royal Commissions and parliamentary committees found that, like the weavers, the miners had established their own culture and identity. Cut off from their 'betters' they created a Welsh working class world of chapels, *friendly societies*, public houses and recreation. About 40 per cent of this population attended chapel regularly, but the *Sunday School* and its obsession with the printed word entered most people's lives.

Many of the first ministers of these *Baptist, Independent,* and *Methodist* chapels were close to the mining families, and were inevitably, if sometimes reluctantly, drawn into their protests. The chapels were also part of the network of self-help that characterized the communities. Everyone was agreed that the working class gave an astonishing amount of assistance to the hungry, the sick and the victimized (E.3). At the same time the mining villages demanded loyalty. 'The workmen almost invariably stick together right or wrong . . .' was a typical comment on the miners of south Wales. When the *Scotch Cattle* or *Chartist* movements were at their height this was not the place to be if one were an outsider, a loner or a *blackleg.*

A much-publicized feature of these working-class communities was their apparent willingness to turn to crime and direct action as a way of surviving. The most industrialized of the Welsh counties were notorious in Britain for the sharp rise in their criminal statistics. The very names of Merthyr Tydfil and Newport were synonymous with violence, drunken behaviour and petty theft. Prize fighting, animal baiting, and boisterous sports added to the atmosphere of a frontier land. For many years these industrial centres were remarkably unpoliced, with only a few parish and works constables supporting the all too few magistrates (E.4). In such places no help could be expected from special constables, military reservists and pensioners. This situation made direct action both more likely and more successful than elsewhere, and the years from 1795 until 1817 saw many acts of 'collective bargaining by riot'. Magistrates, who were themselves often industrial employers, or clergymen, pleaded with governments for the additional protection of troops of soldiers, and the siting of a new military barracks at Brecon gave them a little confidence.

About this time, late in the *Napoleonic Wars,* the first reports appear of a secret society amongst the Monmouthshire iron-workers. Its character is uncertain, but it probably played a part in the strikes of 1816, 1818 and 1819. There may well have been a link also between this society and the *Scotch Cattle* movement, as *Charles Wilkins* implies. Both were interested in controlling the output of the iron and coal industries, and in determining

E.5   the recruitment and training of workmen (E.5). Ultimately, however, the *Scotch Cattle* became a much wider movement, embracing colliers as well as ironworkers, and having a variety of objectives. The main period of Cattle activity lasted from the long strike of 1822 until the mid-1830s, but, despite the claims of some historians, the organization was still prominent in the winters of 1836–37, 1842–43, 1849–50 and 1857–58. National trade unions never achieved the same popularity on the coalfield.

    The nature of this underground organization remains something of a mystery. Its leader was called 'Lolly', 'Ned' or simply 'the Bull', but it is doubtful if one person ever had real control over the movement. In most districts of the coalfield there was a division or cell of the Cattle. Co-operation between the cells was important, because often the herd of one 'Bull calf' operated in the valley of another. Their use of animals' names, and their practice of dressing up in animal skins, is intriguing. There are obvious parallels with the *'ceffyl pren'* (wooden horse) of rural Wales. The first-generation colliers were adapting the mock trial and mob intimidation of their forefathers to the new
E.5   industrial situation (E.5).

    The most loyal supporters of the Bull were the colliers of Monmouthshire and Breconshire. Since the great strike of 1816 they had become more aggressive and violent than the better paid ironworkers. During the widespread industrial action of 1822, 1830 and 1832 the colliers were again the most important and defiant element. Sometimes, as in 1827, the Cattle confined their activities to one colliery village alone, or even to one mine or works. Only one area seems to have largely escaped their attention, and that, contrary to the account of *Charles Wilkins*, was the iron capital itself, Merthyr Tydfil. There, as we shall see, militant *unionism* and *Radicalism* proved more popular.

    Historians have been as fascinated as contemporaries by the reasons for the loyalty shown to the *Scotch Cattle* in south Wales. The simplest explanation, and least satisfying, is that the organization was a Mafia-like movement which was imposed on a fearful population by thugs and criminals. In fact, the organization grew out of the difficult economic and social

E.3

conditions described by the Reverend T. Davies of Llanhilleth in Source E.3. The problems of employment, and the system of paying the men through the *company* or *truck shops*, deprived the colliers of the independence necessary to establish strong trade unions. The power of the employers in this situation was considerable, although perhaps the most hated men were their agents or 'doggies' who cut wages to the bone, took on unskilled workmen, and leased the *company shops*. Outsiders, whether Irish or English, were also unwelcome in bad economic times, as were landlords and bailiffs who *distrained* on the property of indebted miners. The new working class soon realized that the only way to prevent such exploitation was for everyone to be subject to 'the *Scotch Law*'.

In industrial disputes the main role of the Cattle was to maintain discipline. In order to achieve this, they followed a procedure which can be clearly seen in the records. When a strike was called, representatives of the Bull appeared at the mass meetings of workmen. As the days and weeks passed, these hillside gatherings grew more militant, with angry speeches against employers, agents, *blacklegs* and colleagues at neighbouring works. To reinforce their message, the Bull's supporters fired off guns, blew horns and beat drums. On occasions this noise alone proved sufficient, for apprehensive working miners knew the next step in the Cattle's campaign.

E.6

This next step was the sending of threatening letters and the posting up of warning notices (E.6) addressed to three colliers at Clydach, in Breconshire, on 17 June 1823. It was part of an attempt to prevent an early return to work during a strike over piece-work. It was, like so many of the death threats sent to workmen, remarkably effective. Such letters were rarely delivered, so far as we know, to the great employers of the region, possibly because the Cattle realized the contempt with which they would be received. Instead, in an effort to influence their masters and bring works to a complete halt, the colliers' organization attacked company property. Tools, pit-props and engines were popular targets, but the greatest publicity was given to the destruction of coal wagons, barges and tram roads. The best example of this occurred during the three-month strike of 1822. In this protest against severe wage reductions and the

E.7 truck system, the colliers were determined to halt production at all the works along the heads of the south Wales valleys (E.7).

The best known of the Cattle's activities was 'the midnight visit'. The unfortunate victim, who had annoyed the Cattle in some way, was awoken by the noise of a horn and chains, but if he were lucky only a window would be smashed and a red cross left on his door. If he remained disloyal to the strikers or to the wider community, the gangs of disguised colliers would pay him a second visit, this time destroying furniture and belongings. The truly obdurate targets, like Thomas Rees, company shopkeeper and outspoken opponent of working-class activism, were dragged from locked bedrooms and given a beating. In the account of this attack, an informer describes how the Cattle took some of Rees's money; this was rare, for, contrary to much historical opinion, the Bull was not a common thief or

E.8 murderer (E.8).

The evidence given by the informer, John Jones, in the Monmouthshire Assizes of 1835, is an indication that the colliers' organization was losing some of its remarkable discipline and loyalty. Until this time it was virtually impossible to obtain witnesses who would stand against the Cattle in court. Parish and special constables were afraid of the anger of the community, and magistrates did not act decisively until 1834. Then, with the encouragement of central government, magistrates and employers came together, outlawed combinations of all kinds, and set up a temporary armed force of 'mountain

E.9 police' (E.9). The breakthrough came almost immediately, for a woman was accidentally killed in a Cattle raid, and three men were sentenced to death for her murder. Despite the jury's plea

E.10 for mercy, one of them, Edward Morgan, was hanged (E.10). His execution has always been regarded as the end of the movement's dominance, but the Cattle continued to be an unwelcome element in industrial relations until national unions were well established.

The mid-1830s proved to be a fruitful period in the development of the working-class consciousness. The Reform crisis of 1830–32 changed the traditional scope of electoral contests, and allowed 'the people' onto the political stage. At

Merthyr, Carmarthen and Newtown there was serious rioting on behalf of 'Reform', and even the *Scotch Cattle* took up the slogan. Just as important was the emergence of an élite of ultra-radicals, men like Hugh Williams, the Carmarthen solicitor, John Frost, the Newport draper, and Morgan Williams, the master weaver of Merthyr Tydfil. The events of the next few years confirmed their predictions about the inadequacies of moderate reform, and put them at the head of a working-class

E.11   movement committed to democratic politics. In Source E.11 John Frost offers the usual criticism of the reformed Parliament, and, in particular, attacks the *Poor Law Amendment Act* of 1834 which was so unpopular in the Principality, not least amongst the weavers of Montgomeryshire.

Although the *People's Charter* was not published until the late spring of 1838, the campaign for democratic rights in Wales began early in the previous year with the formation of a *Working Men's Association* in Carmarthen. It was quickly followed by the establishment of three similar bodies in the main weaving towns of mid-Wales. The driving forces for political change were Hugh Williams, his friend William Jenkins, Newtown iron-monger Thomas Powell, and an elusive character, the heavy-drinking Charles Jones of Welshpool. Hugh Williams was active at this time on the south Wales coalfield, but his contribution to its first political society, formed at Pontypool in July 1837, was probably small. Like so many of the earliest radical associations, the one in Pontypool was led by tradesmen and craftsmen rather than by workers in heavy industry. At Newport, where a society appeared in the summer of 1838, the key men were the massive baker, William Edwards, and two radical veterans, the printer Samuel Etheridge and the draper, John Frost. Frost, along with Hugh Williams and Charles Jones, was nominated to represent the Welsh constituencies at the first *Chartist* convention in 1839.

E.14   The nature of the *Chartist* message is clear from Source E.14. Their analysis of the evils of society and their remedy for change was essentially political. The Swansea *Working Men's Association*, and others like it, argued that the aristocracy of land and money had grabbed power in Britain, and kept their monopoly by dominating Parliament and the electorate. The people had

Contemporary drawing of a Chartist meeting. (*Source: The Mansell Collection.*)

been denied basic human rights, including the right to enjoy the fruits of one's labour. Working people, it was claimed, had produced enormous wealth in Wales over these decades, and yet remained surprisingly poor. The only solution to such inequality was not the intimidation of the *Scotch Cattle*, nor the short-term rewards of trade *unionism*, but for the people to seize political power. This was a sophisticated message that was well received in many parts of Britain.

The best way to obtain such radical reform caused more debate. As we can see from Sources E.12 and E.14 the Swansea and Carmarthen *Chartists* did not expect too much help from other classes. It was better to educate the working class in democratic politics, and to build a great national movement on their support. Contrary to the views of most historians, it is evident that all radicals believed both in the value of such education or 'moral force', and in the sad but ultimate necessity of 'physical force' if all else failed. As Hugh Williams makes clear, their great hope, and expectation, was that the class unity won by education, meetings, petitions and conventions would prove irresistible (E.14). They were soon to discover their mistake.

Whilst the optimism lasted, there were hundreds of *Chartist* sympathizers all over Wales; they bought copies of the *Northern Star* and *Western Vindicator* in 1839, and a few of the keenest democrats even welcomed the last of the *Chartist* lecturers twenty years later. Yet radical organizations flourished in only a few regions of the Principality. In the weaving towns of mid-Wales several hundred people enrolled in political unions and associations, and a number of these were said to be in favour of armed resistance. However, the researches of historians David Williams and Owen Ashton reveal that the Chartist Rising at Llanidloes, which began late in April 1839, was a misnomer; it was more of an anti-police demonstration, sparked off by the antics of the ex-mayor Thomas Marsh, and used by the authorities as an excuse to beat the *Chartists* (E.15). In general, the leadership of mid-Wales *Radicalism* was remarkable for its discipline and loyalty. As late as 1858 Llanidloes and Newtown were represented in the last *Chartist* conference, and they dutifully established a branch of the National Reform League.

E.12
E.14

E.14

E.15

In north Wales there were groups of radicals at Bangor, Caernarfon, Holywell, and Overton, but *Chartist* lecturers were never able to convert the interest shown by colliers at Mold, Buckley and Wrexham into long-lasting organizations. In the south-western counties it was a similar story; although radical meetings were held in the late 1830s at Narberth, Haverford-west, Fishguard, Pembroke and other places, it proved difficult, outside the Carmarthen neighbourhood, to keep the *Chartist* flame alive.

For a time at least it seemed that the south Wales coalfield was at the front of the democratic movement in Britain. After a slow start, the work of William Edwards and missionary Henry Vincent began to bear fruit. In the late winter of 1838–39 thousands of miners bought *Chartist* cards, and by the following summer perhaps 25,000 men and women had enrolled in associations. This was community politics on an unprecedented scale, and was rightly compared with the achievement of the *Chartist* weavers of the West Riding. After their leaders were arrested in the late spring, and meetings banned, the south Wales miners made promises of *Scotch Cattle*-type revenge and talked of revolution. Parliament's dismissal of the great *Chartist* Petition in the summer, and the collapse of the People's Convention soon afterwards, only increased the sense of frustration, and leading militants demanded that Frost carry out his part of a national conspiracy to overthrow the government.

It has now been established that the events of 3–4 November at Newport were a genuine attempt at a rising, for which John Frost, Zephaniah Williams and William Jones narrowly escaped the punishment of death. The midnight march of 7–8000 miners, many of them armed to the teeth, was the most serious insurrectionary movement in nineteenth-century Britain (E.16). The inevitable anticlimax, and discrediting of physical-force methods, has caused some historians to neglect the later *Chartist* story. By 1842 the *Chartist* movement had recovered its popularity on the coalfield. Merthyr Tydfil, now the heart of Welsh *Radicalism*, proved to be exceptionally loyal to the cause; in 1842 thousands signed another petition and hundreds came out in support of the general strike. The strike lasted for only a short time at Merthyr, but for a while Morgan Williams and his

E.16

friends were able to persuade hungry miners that *Chartist*
E.17   demands were as important as higher wages (E.17).
        After 1842 the radical movement lost something of its mass
        appeal, although there was more support for *Feargus O'Connor's*
E.18   *Land Plan* in south Wales than David Williams suggested
        (E.18). In 1848, the year of revolutions, the *Chartists* again took
        to the streets, causing exaggerated alarm. With some exceptions
        the working class no longer felt it necessary to join political
        unions. The *Chartist* associations at Merthyr were kept alive
        through the 1850s by artisans like Henry Thomas, the cooper,
        and William Gould, the grocer. In time they were drawn into
        Liberal politics, helping to organize working-class support for
        the parliamentary candidate, *Henry Richard*, during his election
        triumph of 1868. The irony of this is obvious, for just as the
        Chartists sought to raise people's horizons above the level of
        popular violence, so *Nonconformist* Liberals like Richard tried to
        detach working-class democrats from their dreams of an
        egalitarian revolution. It was time to forget the class hostility
E.19   and ambitions that we have been describing in this essay (E.19).

Sources

Class Consciousness, Social Conditions, and Solidarity.

E.1   His (the Welsh workman) social sphere becomes one of
       complete isolation from all influences, save such as arises with
       his own order . . . He is left to live in an under-world of his
       own, and the march of society goes so completely over his head,
       that he is never heard of, excepting when the strange and
       abnormal features of a Revival, or a Rebecca or *Chartist*
       outbreak, call attention to a phase of society which could
       produce anything so contrary to all that we elsewhere
       experience.

       (Ralph R. W. Lingen, *Report on the State of Education in Wales*,
       1847, Part I, p.3.)

E.2   Except in a few of the works the relations between employers
       and employed was of the worst description. Next to nothing
       was done for the comfort and convenience of life among the

work-people; . . . Except in a few places the schools were a nullity. There were no possibilities of amusements or comfort out of doors or in it. The houses were greatly overcrowded with lodgers . . . Nearly the whole body of employers acted on Bentham's theory that the masters had no responsibility beyond paying the men their wages; everything else that they wanted the men had to do for themselves . . . The men and their wives were astonished at the idea that the Government wanted to know all about them, and that sympathy existed anywhere towards them. Their ignorance was pitiable . . . One of the principal Dissenting Ministers in one district, who endeavoured to open their minds (against *Chartism*), nearly lost his life.

(E. L. and O. P. Edmonds, eds., *I was there: the Memoirs of H. S. Tremenheere*, 1965, pp.37–8.)

E.3   This parish (of Llanhilleth, Monmouthshire), is an agricultural district, interspersed with small collieries, which are super-intended by petty agents or foremen (the owners being non-resident). Here the collier is not employed except at such times as there is a demand for coal in the market (Newport) . . . as a general rule, it may be said that he is unemployed for 10 days in each month; . . . During the interval of non-employment, they are supported by getting credit in small country (truck) shops, who sell inferior goods at an extravagantly high price, and thus they become involved in debt, of which they can never finally discharge . . .

There is another evil connected with the condition of the operative in this district . . . the practice of agents keeping public-houses.

The work people are very kind to each other, and will help each other in times of distress to an extent that would scarcely be believed, and ought to put to shame the paltry charity of those who are in wealthy circumstances.

(The Reverend T. Davies, *Report on the State of Education in Wales*, 1847, Part II, pp.299–300.)

E.4   It may be worthwhile to observe that the manner in which the Hill population of Monmouthshire and Glamorganshire has increased of late years resembles the growth of a penal settlement as well as of a prosperous manufacturing district. Whenever a man runs away from his family or commits any depredation in . . . the adjoining counties the answer to any enquiry is, 'he has gone to the Hills'. There, without any police worth speaking of to watch newcomers, or control the resident bad characters, the whole mass of the Welsh, Irish, runaway criminals and vagrants has fermented together, until this outbreak (the *Newport rising*) has demonstrated of what material it consists.

(Home Office Papers, 73/55. Letter from Edmund Head, 14 November 1839.)

Scotch Cattle

E.5 All through the Peninsular Campaign the works were more or less the scene of disquietude. Illegal action was common, and in no way more strikingly shown than by the origin of bands known as the '*Scotch Cattle*'.

It is many years since those lawless days were to the fore. An old inhabitant not many years ago recalled them with a shudder. He said: 'I was but young then, but the very mention of the likelihood that the *Scotch Cattle* were coming that night put me into a fever. The *Scotch Cattle* were bands of men enrolled privately in most of the ironwork towns, with the object first of restricting the output of minerals, and thereby keeping up prices of iron and wages of miners. One of the laws was that no stranger should be taught mining . . . At all events, nothing should be done without the sanction of the Society, . . . The means adopted for carrying out the rules of the Society were principally personal violence.'

(Charles Wilkins, *The History of the Iron, Steel, Tinplate, and Other Trades of Wales*, 1903, p.178.)

E.6 How many times we gave notice to you about going in to work before you settle all together to go on better terms than were before and better than what you ask at present?

Notice to you David Thomas John, and David Davies, and
Andrew Cross, that the Bull and his friends are all alive, and the
vale of Llamarch is wide, and woe shall be to you, since death
you shall doubtless have all at once, you may depend on this. It
may be that the night you do not expect, we shall come again.
We are not afraid were you to go all at once to work.

(English version of a mixed Welsh and English notice. J. Lloyd,
The Early History of the Old South Wales Iron Works, 1760–1840,
1906, p.195.)

E.7   It seems that arrangements were made for conveying some
waggons of coal from Crumlin Wharf at the head of the
Monmouthshire Canal to the iron-works of Messrs Harford and
Co. at Ebbw Vale, ten miles higher up the country. The
Chepstow Cavalry, under the command of Capt. Buckle, were at
Crumlin by eight o'clock, accompanied by several of the
neighbouring Magistrates; and the Scots Greys were sent from
Abergavenny . . .

About two miles . . . above Llanhilleth, the mob came down,
having obstructed the convoy by tearing up the roads and
running several waggons across them. They made a most
desperate attack on this part of the convoy, and a most confused
scene of riot and disorder ensued, and Mr Frere, the Magistrate,
was knocked off his horse. The Greys fired a volley over the
heads of the rioters, but chiefly used their swords, and several
wounds were inflicted; . . . The convoy was at last able to
proceed, but slowly, . . .

Notwithstanding the number of rioters wounded, and some
very severely, others of them during the night destroyed or
disabled about twenty wagons which . . . had been left near the
Monmouthshire Canal Company's reservoir at Llanhilleth: . . .
the coals (more than two tons in each wagon) were set on fire,
and, with every thing combustible about the waggons, totally
consumed, . . .

(*The Cambrian*, 11 and 18 May 1822.)

E.8   They told him (John James) . . . if he would consent to go with
them, his wife and children should be provided for, in case

he got into any trouble; . . . they disguised themselves by
blackening their faces, and some put on portions of women's
clothes; . . . they broke into the house (of Thomas Rees) and
destroyed the furniture with a sledge; . . . a man named Edward
Howell set fire to the curtain and took it upstairs, and he had
heard that it was a man named Blainey who beat Mr Rees; . . . an
iron-chest was thrown downstairs, which was immediately
smashed with the sledge, and a scramble took place for the
money, he himself only getting 4*s*. . . :

(Confession of John James, Monmouthshire Assizes, *The*
Cambrian, 11 April 1835.)

E.9   Resolved unanimously,
        That it is the determination of this meeting not to employ
        hereafter any man who is engaged in any Trades Union Society
        or in any other association not sanctioned by law, and that every
        Proprietor of Works will issue notice . . . to that effect, and
        further that they will not at any time hereafter employ any
        person who may be found to assist in or give countenance to the
        outrages committed against the persons or property of their
        workmen by miscreants who assemble at night under the
        denomination of *Scotch Cattle*.

(Home Office Papers, 52/25. Meeting of magistrates and
employers in the south Wales iron and coal industries, 13 June
1834.)

E.10   *Execution at Monmouth*
        On Monday last, the awful and revolting scene of an execution,
        which has been, fortunately, of such rare occurrence for years at
        Monmouth, was witnessed, at the front of our county gaol, by
        from three to four thousand spectators. Edward Morgan, found
        guilty, . . . contrary to the expectations of a crowded court, of
        the murder of Joan Thomas, at the parish of Bedwellty, in a
        Scotch Cattle riot, received the last sentence of the law in a state
        of pitiable agitation; . . .
        Morgan made a confession . . . He admitted being present
        with the gang of rioters on the night of the attack on Thomas
        Thomas' house, but declared that they induced him by threats to

TO
JOHN FROST, Esq,

One of her Majesty's Justices of the Peace for the Borough of Newport,
Monmouthshire.

SIR,

The Working Men's Association respectfully request, that you will convene a Public Meeting of the Inhabitants of Newport, to take into consideration the principles contained in the People's Charter, and to consider the propriety of adopting the National Petition. The Association request that you will preside at the Meeting.

Association Room, October 23rd, 1838.

By order of the Meeting.

In compliance with the request of the Association, I convene a Public Meeting of the Inhabitants of Newport and Pill, for the purposes stated in the requisition, to be holden in the large room at the PARROT INN, on *Tuesday Evening*, the 30th of October; I will take the chair at 7 o'clock precisely.   JOHN FROST.

Newport, October 25th, 1838.

To the Tradesmen of Newport.

TOWNSMEN.

Much of the evils of life proceeds from ignorant, corrupt, and oppressive men in authority. The object of the Working Men's Association, is, to place in the House of Commons able, honest, and industrious men. Is there a Tradesman in Newport who ought not to endeavour to further this object? Is there a Tradesman who would not be benefited could this design be effected? One Thousand Pounds a week are taken from this town in general taxes, would it be to the disadvantage of the Inhabitants if the one half were retained? What are the Tradesmen afraid that they would become too rich? Do they apprehend danger were they to keep the fruits of their labour? What has the Reform produced? There are the same men sitting in the House as sat there before the Reform bill passed, and the nation sees the same measures. Does any man expect that members put into the House of Commons by bribery, perjury, violence, drunkenness, will make laws favourable to the people? A bad system cannot produce good men, and the powerful Associations formed, and forming all over the kingdom intend to change the system. They do not look for Figs from Thistles. If the Tradesmen of Newport are favourable to the principles contained in the National Petition they will support it; if they believe that to pass the People's Charter would be injurious to the community, they will now have an opportunity of shewing its evil tendency. The time is fast approaching when there must be no neutrals; .the question will be, who is for good and cheap Government, and who is against it. I respectfully, cordially invite the Tradesmen of Newport to support the principles contained in the People's Charter, or to shew that they are wrong.

I am, faithfully your obedient Servant,

JOHN FROST.

John Partridge, Printer, Newport.

John Frost's broadsheet supporting the People's Charter. (*Source: Newport Central Library.*)

join them; he did not fire the gun by which Joan Thomas was killed, being about twenty yards from the person who so fired, which he (Morgan) said was done without any intention of murder; . . . He hoped that his ruin would be useful in teaching bad men to shun those *combinations* which brought him to an ignominious death, and that content would be restored amongst the working classes.

(*Monmouthshire Merlin*, 11 April 1835.)

Chartism

E.11   Reform is once more the order of the day — . . . They had found out that the Reform Bill was humbug — it was intended for nothing else. They had had Reform for nearly eight years, and what was the effect? . . . Ten thousand had been added to the standing army . . . we have had the *Irish Coercion Bill* . . . the *Dorchester affair*; all these have resulted from *Whig* domination.

One oppressive act follows the other. Some time ago we had the *Poor-law Amendment Act*, by which the management of your own money was completely taken out of your own hands, . . . Here's a pretty law, by which poverty is made a crime and punishment by confinement, by a separation of man and wife, and parent and child. To support this oppressive law we now have a rural police! — armed men all over the country — to suppress discontent by force, . . .

(John Frost, declarations published in the *Monmouthshire Merlin*, 3 November 1838, and the *Western Vindicator*, 26 October 1839.)

E.12   A general meeting of the members (of the Carmarthen Working Men's Association) was held on this day, . . . Mr H. Williams, the secretary, . . . first of all explained the principles of free (universal) *suffrage*, as being an inherent civil right, that ought to create the Government; . . . it was incumbent on the friends of the cause to press it also on the aristocratic and middle-class representatives of the country:— but, and to mark that, for its ultimate success to depend upon themselves, on their own class alone, . . .

(Report of a meeting on 3 April 1837, Lovett MSS, City of Birmingham Central Reference Library, vol. 1, p.48.)

E.13 Mr Hugh Williams, of Carmarthen, then stood forward. Brother Radicals (he said), I appear before you this day on behalf of your brother radicals of south Wales . . . They are prepared to assert their rights . . . I do not mean to say that moral force alone will secure those rights. We require physical force, but how is that to be obtained? It is organization we require. By acting in unison we shall obtain one object.

(Speech at Palace Yard, Westminster, 17 September 1838. Lovett MSS, vol. 1, p.250.)

E.14 We seek to establish a popular and just government,— to render the source of justice pure and incorruptible,— to obtain for the people a voice in the enactment of laws . . .

We would have you remember, that labour creates capital, (but) . . . you lie at the mercy of those whose wealth you have laboured to produce. You produce capital, and crawl to it; you make a golden calf, and bow down to it . . .

In most parts of England, Scotland and Wales, the oppressed multitudes have become sensible of the enormity of the system which has so long ground them into the dust, and are making the most strenuous efforts to recover their rights as human beings: while their rulers are studying the arts of oppression, they are making themselves acquainted with the principles of good government; acquiring and spreading political knowledge, by means of associations; they are preparing a petition to Parliament for the restoration of their acknowledged rights; they have appointed a number of delegates to meet in convention to watch over and urge the petition . . .

(Address of the Swansea *Working Men's Association*. March 1839.)

E.15 As soon as (the crowd) came within hearing, they shouted out that three of their comrades had been arrested in front of the hotel (Trewythen Arms, Llanidloes) by the London police . . .

When their request (for their release) was denied them, the mob set up a terrible shout, and pressed forward towards the door of the inn; the rioters asserting that the London police began the conflict by striking one of their number . . . They further state that the Ex-Mayor, on finding that he was locked out, to ensure his own safety, suddenly appeared to sympathize with the mob, by crying out '*Chartists* for ever'; and, with a stick which he had in his hand, broke the first pane of glass, thus initiating the mob in the work of destruction.

The women followed the example thus set them by throwing stones at every window of the house, . . . Guns were next fired through the door, which after resisting all their efforts for some time, was ultimately burst open. The mob quickly spread themselves over the house in search of their comrades, whom they found handcuffed in the kitchen. They were at once led off to a smith's shop, where their gyves [foot shackles] were knocked off.

(Edward Hamer, *A Brief Account of the Chartist Outbreak in Llanidloes*, 1867, pp. 17–18.)

E.16   At least eight thousand men, mostly miners employed in the neighbourhood (which is very densely populated) were engaged in the attack upon the town of Newport and . . . many of them were armed. Their design seems to have been to wreak their vengeance upon the Newport magistrates, for the prosecution of Vincent and others, now lying in Monmouth gaol, and after securing the town, to advance to Monmouth, and liberate these prisoners. The ultimate design of the leaders does not appear; but it probably was to rear the standard of rebellion throughout Wales, in hopes of being able to hold the royal forces at bay, in that mountainous district, until the people of England, assured by successes, should rise en masse, for the same objects. According to the evidence now before the world, Mr Frost, the late member of the Convention, led the rioters, and he, with others, has been committed for high treason. On entering Newport, the people marched straight to the Westgate Hotel, where the magistrates, with about 40 soldiers were assembled, being fully apprised of the intended outbreak. The

Riot Act was read, and the soldiers fired down, with ease and security, upon the people who had first broken and fired into the windows . . . About thirty of the people are known to have been killed, and several to have been wounded.

(Report in the *Charter*, 17 November 1839.)

E.17 The movement at Merthyr Tydfil is entirely political, and under the direction of Morgan Williams, the Clothier, who has been a notorious leader of the *Chartist*s for some time past. He receives his instructions daily from the North, and the cry is 'now or never' . . . The state of wages is a mere pretence, as indeed is evident from the contradictory speeches of some of the local agitators. It appears that few of the workmen, hitherto, have been induced to quit their work, except the colliers connected with the *Cyfarthfa Works* and the *Penydarren Works*, and some in the Aberdare Valley. These people will soon return unless the strike in the North is kept up.

(Home Office Papers, 45/265B. Letter from the Marquis of Bute, 23 August 1842.)

E.18 MERTHYR TYDFIL. — . . . Mr Manning, of Cardiff, . . . lectured to the members of No.1 branch (of the National Land Company), on 'the Land and its capabilities'. He was loudly applauded. Mr Manning delivered a second lecture on the Charter . . .

— The tea party of the second branch came off, on Christmas eve. The attendance was very encouraging; John Emerys Jones was voted to the chair. Several toasts were given; amongst others were 'Long life to the star of redemption, Feargus O'Connor, Esq.', 'Success to his mission' (and) 'The Emancipation of Labour'. On Monday evening the committee reassembled, when steps were taken to obtain signatures to the Land petition.

(*Northern Star*, 4 December 1847, and 1 January 1848.)

E.19 For the last hundred or hundred and fifty years there is probably no part of the United Kingdom that has given the authorities so little trouble or anxiety. Anything like sedition, tumult, or riot is very rare in the Principality. There have been only two exceptions (the *Newport rising* and the Rebecca Riots) to this rule, and these have been more apparent than real . . . the *Chartist* outbreak in Newport in 1839 . . . was almost entirely of English inspiration, . . . The great bulk of the Welsh people had no share whatever in the movement, but looked upon it with undisguised repugnance and horror.

(Henry Richard, *Letters and Essays on Wales*, 1866, reprinted 1884, pp.81–82.)

Debating the Evidence

In this essay, Dr David Jones deals with the types of evidence which historians use to enter the world of working-class experience and activity in the first half of the nineteenth century. In researching such questions as the activities of the *Scotch Cattle* and the motives of the *Chartists* who marched on Newport in 1839, the historian of nineteenth-century Wales is faced with two major difficulties. In the first place there is the problem of the availability of evidence and, where the evidence does exist, the limitations imposed upon the historian by its imperfect and fragmentary nature. Despite the gradual spread of education in the nineteenth century, the high level of illiteracy meant that the evidence from working people themselves is limited. In addition, the very nature of movements such as the *Scotch Cattle* and the activities of the 'physical force' *Chartists*, necessitated that they either did not keep records themselves or they destroyed them. Therefore in an attempt to enter this hidden world, historians such as David Jones have to extract what material they can from a wide variety of sources. Then, of course, the historian is faced by the second major problem of the *reliability* of evidence. This is true of all the sources used by Dr Jones, but it is particularly the case in his use of two particular types of source — newspapers and the records of official enquiries carried out by Parliamentary Committees and Royal Commissions. Extensive use of these sources is made by historians throughout this volume and there are two reasons for this. First, whilst neither was a completely new type of historical evidence, each proliferated considerably in the nineteenth century. On the one hand, increasing literacy created a demand for newspapers and periodicals and, on the other, despite the prevalence of *laissez-faire* ideas, the reformed system of government in Britain did exhibit a growing inclination to enquire into the effect of the sweeping changes which industrialization was bringing about. Secondly, these sources do allow much greater insight into working-class experience than might otherwise be possible. The evidence given to official enquiries, the reports of the Government investigator, the eyewitness accounts of journalists and the newspaper articles written by a working-class *Chartist* all take us much closer to *lived* experience. However, as will be realized, the use the historian makes of such sources must be rigorous and critical.

Source E.1
Immediately we see the necessity for rigorous critical appraisal. Here is an extract from the notorious *Blue Books of 1847*, which, to *Nonconformists* in Wales in particular, were to be seen as treasonous to the Welsh people — *Brad y Llyfrau Gleision*. Why, on the basis of this extract, should this be? What would you need to know about how this evidence was collected, and in particular about Ralph Lingen, before you could make use of this source?

Source E.2
What does Dr Jones tell us about how this source originated and what bearing does this have on its worth as evidence? How do you explain the date given here and what would you need to establish about the original dating of the source and why?

Source E.3
What features of this testimony which may have been taken for granted at the time could be revealing to the modern reader? What does this informant mean by 'the evil' of 'agents keeping public-houses'? How far would the informant's profession have some bearing on how we value this statement?

Source E.4
Why is it important to establish who Edmund Head is and why he wrote to the Home Office? What weakness does his evidence appear to have?

Source E.5

On what grounds could you argue that this is *not* a primary source for the activities of *Scotch Cattle*?

Sources E.6 and E.8

Dr Jones mentions in his essay the possibility that the kinds of actions depicted in these sources may have had their origins in the Welsh countryside. Is there any evidence in the sources used by Dr David Howell to support this view?

Source E.7

Are there any indications that this report is not based on firsthand experience of the events described? What phrases suggest a possible bias on the part of the journalist or the newspaper's editor?

Source E.8

Why would it be useful to try to establish why John James made this confession? What bearing might answers to such a question have on the reliability of his evidence? Does any particular part of what John James says lead you to question the overall reliability of the source?

Source E.9

Why might it be important to discover how and for what reasons this document found its way into the records of the Home Office? What other kinds of sources might help to establish the authenticity of this evidence?

Source E.10

What questions do we need to ask of a newspaper source such as this before we are able to assess its reliability? What aspects of Edward Morgan's confession are *not* made clear here?

Sources E.5–E.10

Considering these sources as a whole what evidence do they provide about the activities of the *Scotch Cattle*? Which of these sources do you feel to be the most reliable for this purpose and which the least reliable?

Source E.11

What do you consider to be the strengths and weaknesses of this source?

What specific criticisms does John Frost make of the *Poor Law Amendment Act*?

Source E.12
In what respect is Hugh Williams's argument for electoral reform here different from that made by John Frost in Source E.11? This source is taken from the papers of William Lovett, the London radical who was one of the founders of the *Chartist* movement. What would you need to know before accepting this as a reliable account of what Hugh Williams said in Carmarthen?

Source E.13
This source provides evidence on the major debate within the *Chartist* movement. What, do you deduce, was this debate? What does Hugh Williams have to say on it? Source E.12 will also help you in deciding upon Williams's position.

Source E.14
What phrases and images in the source clearly reflect its bias? What bearing might speculation on the authorship of this source have on our understanding of the nature of *Chartism* in Wales at the time?

Source E.15
What would you need to know about this source and its author before you could be sure it was primary evidence for the Llanidloes disturbances of 1839? What phrases in the extract suggest a possible bias on Edward Hamer's part? What accusation does Hamer make against the ex-mayor of the town and does he make this accusation on the basis of firsthand evidence?

Source E.16
This *Chartist* paper deals here with the reasons it believes to have been behind the *Chartist* march on Newport in November 1839. What do you think may be the strengths and weaknesses of the source?

Source E.17
What is the Marquis of Bute arguing here are the reasons for the strike of 1842 in Merthyr Tydfil? What phrases or references suggest bias on his part? What other evidence might you consult on this question?

Source E.18

What two points made about *Chartism* after 1839, in David Jones's essay, are illustrated here?

Source E.19

Select two examples from David Jones's sources and two more from Merfyn Jones's sources which appear to contradict what Henry Richard is arguing here. A longer extract from this source (including this passage) can be seen in Source B.8. What additional points about *Chartism* in Wales does *Henry Richard* make there?

Discussion

We return now to crucial questions which we must ask of David Jones's sources as a whole and in particular his use of newspapers and official reports and enquiries. A third of his sources are extracts from newspapers. *The Cambrian*, the first English-language newspaper in Wales, established in Swansea in 1804, provides two pieces of evidence. In at least one of these (E.7) the language suggests hostility to the supporters of the *Scotch Cattle*. There are two selections from *The Monmouthshire Merlin* (E.10 and E.11), a newspaper owned and published by two notable enemies of *Chartism* — R. J. Blewett and Edward Dowling. Finally there are two extracts from *Chartist* newspapers (E.16 and E.18). Then, as now, newspapers took up political positions. What is less clear is the extent to which bias intrudes into reporting. Equally problematic, however, is assessing the extent to which reportage is based on firsthand evidence. This was particularly queried in E.7 and E.10 and is clearly of concern. What we have to remember is that with all the potential for historical research into the experience of the mass of people which newspapers allow, they are just one more flawed source. Dr Jones uses two extracts from an official enquiry — both taken from the Education *Commissioners'* Report of 1847, which created a furore in Wales. Other historians in this volume make greater use of such material, but the fundamental questions which have to be asked of them emerge clearly from these two extracts. As the question asked of Source E.1 suggests, it is crucial to know the extent to which Lingen's conclusions are based on extensive and representative evidence. Lingen himself, a barrister and a member of the Church of

England, displayed considerable hostility to the language and to many manifestations of *Nonconformity*, the religion of the majority of the Welsh people. In E.3 we return to the theme of the way in which informants were selected to give evidence to Royal Commissions and the reliability of their evidence. Why and how was the Reverend T. Davies chosen; to what extent are we still failing to obtain evidence directly from the people who experienced the conditions the informant describes? As historians attempt to reconstruct the hidden world of working-class experience in newly-industrialized Wales, they are grateful for the availability of sources such as these. But they can never tell the whole story.

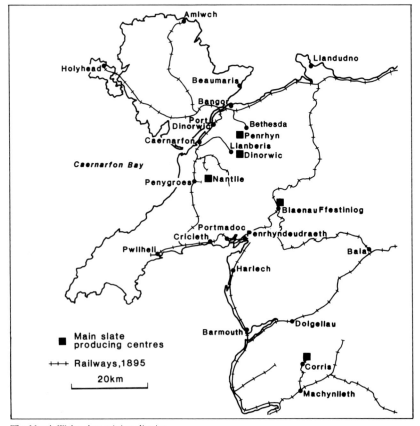

The North Wales slate mining district.

Rural and Industrial Protest in North Wales

MERFYN JONES

The importance of those nervous and agitated years, the 1880s, both in the development of the labour movement in Britain, and in the advance of a radical and nationalist-inclined liberalism in Wales, is widely acknowledged by historians. The decade which witnessed the arrival of an organized socialism in Britain and, later, saw the threatening sight of unemployment riots in London, ended with the sweeping and profound challenge of the mass strikes of previously unorganized 'unskilled' workers in the phenomenon of 'new *unionism*'. Whilst the 'Irish question' dominated political debate and Scotland won a Secretary of State, the Welsh, too, agitated and organized and, particularly after the electoral changes of the mid-decade, there was a surge of Welsh organizational creativity which amounted to a national renaissance: Cymru Fydd, the national wing of liberalism, began on its contradictory and meandering path in 1886, its journal was founded in 1888; the Society for the Utilization of the Welsh Language was founded in 1885; in the following year *Thomas Gee* and his tenant-farmer allies launched an anti-*tithe* organization which, in 1887, became the Welsh Land League. Wales stood largely, though far from unanimously, for Gladstonian Liberalism and Irish Home Rule and new political figures emerged, typified by *Tom Ellis*, the radical son of a tenant farmer who was elected Liberal MP for
F.1   Merioneth in 1886 (F.1). In the General Election of November 1885, the Liberals won thirty of the thirty-four Welsh seats. In the five north Wales counties their victory was even more emphatic and they carried the day in nine out of the ten constituencies — only Denbigh boroughs remained in *Tory* hands.

This Liberal triumph, and the associated construction of a *Nonconformist* and radical tradition which aspired to hegemonic influence in Wales, has been much discussed, particularly in its effects on the formal business of representative politics, and historians have traced the roots of this process to earlier developments in the 1850s and 1860s. The 1880s witnessed the political triumph of forces which had long been active, particularly in the politics of religious denominationalism. The apparent unanimity of Welsh politics, which observers found so striking; the confluence of cultural, religious and political currents which opponents found so disabling; these are now seen as being the results of earlier developments, brought to fruition by the extension of the franchise in 1885.

But radical influence and re-definition were not limited to the political arena: they seemed to be affecting economic relationships as well. North Wales was in a remarkably disturbed state by the 1880s as tenant farmers and quarrymen sought to re-define their relationships with their masters and employers. Popular, and often violent, mass protest became a feature of the north Wales countryside and was present, too, in the region's major industry — quarrying and mining. The *Tithe War* of 1886–8 and the strikes in Llanddulas, near Abergele, in 1885–6 and in Llanberis in the same year gave north Wales a national reputation for unrest and disturbed social conditions (F.2). The presence of the military ensured a high visibility for these mass protests and journalists from London papers as different as *The Times* and the Marxist *Justice* journeyed to north Wales to witness the excitement (F.3). The visit of Michael Davitt, the much-imprisoned Irish land-reformer, to the area in 1886 seemed to confirm the view that north Wales was moving towards agitation on an Irish scale. Many of the ingredients seemed familiar: calls for land reform, religious sectarianism, a tendency toward direct action and calls for specifically Welsh remedies to what were perceived as Welsh problems.

At the service of quarrymen and tenant farmers were a band of able and influential organizers and propagandists such as *W.J. Parry* of Bethesda, who had his finger in a bewildering number of Welsh causes and newpapers, and *Thomas Gee*, who had forged his *Baner ac Amserau Cymru* into a powerful Welsh

F.2

F.3

voice from his citadel in Denbigh. These men, and many others, businessmen, journalists, ministers of religion, used the power of their words to depict north Wales as a land sorely oppressed by Anglican landlordism actively engaged in the persecution of an impoverished and *Nonconformist* people. They defined a view of Wales, and of north Wales in particular, which constrained Welsh culture for generations. Welsh writers and politicians — and historians, too — operated within the touchstones of this portrayal: the vocabulary of the Welsh language itself seemed incapable of delineating alternative visions (F.4).

F.4

Those who did not adhere to this Welsh 'world-view' observed these developments in disbelief. They regularly took the claims of radicals, expounded and rehearsed weekly in a clutch of newspapers, examined them, threw statistics and logic at them, but they could not dispel them. In 1886 they formed the North Wales Property Defence Association to counter 'the incessant interference of outside agitators'. Finally, the campaigns of the 1880s led to the Royal Commission on Land in Wales and Monmouthshire which reported in 1896: two world views clashed, and at length. Landowners and radicals presented their statistics, but also elaborated them endlessly with different passions and notions of 'rights'.

Historians have at last started to take the claims of landlordism seriously and to subject them to critical analysis. The evidence seems to suggest that Welsh landlords were not as vicious nor as incompetent as they have often been portrayed; on the contrary it appears that the larger the landowners the more enlightened were their policies. This is a complete reversal of the view put forward by the reformers for whom the larger the landowner the larger was his guilt. In an attempt, therefore, to explain the agitations of the 1880s some historians have emphasized the validity of the landowners' claim that it had all been got up by radical agitators; that the Land Question was no more than 'a figment of the political imagination'. This was what *Lord Penrhyn*, one of the largest land and quarry owners, and his allies consistently claimed: that the quarrymen had been a contented workforce until organized into a union by a group of *Nonconformist*, middle-class Liberals; that tenants and farmers had lived peaceably with their masters until a deluge of

F.5   incitement and propaganda overwhelmed the countryside in the
       1880s (F.5). In this analysis neither quarrymen nor tenant
       farmers are seen as having had serious grievances; they were all
       manufactured by an aspirant group of outsiders. The proven-
       ance of protest, it was alleged, was the newpaper column and
       the pulpit.

This is a serious analysis and it is interesting to note that historians have finally been able to investigate further than the flood of radical invective published in pamphlets, books and newspapers, and study estate and other records which show a different picture. But does the available evidence support this conspiracy analysis? And, if not, what are its limitations?

To take the quarrying industry first: the two strikes which attracted the greatest attention in the 1880s were those in the limestone quarries in Llanddulas, when the military had to be brought in to protect *blackleg* workers from Liverpool, and in the great slate quarries of Dinorwig in Llanberis in Caernarfonshire when some 2,700 men were locked out for five weeks in a crucial power struggle between men and master. Both strikes attracted considerable sympathy from a wide range of Welsh opinion and the men's case was regularly advocated in local newspapers, but in no sense can it be argued that in either case was the strike caused by political initiative, although each was often interpreted in such a way. On the contrary, close investigation shows that the middle-class leadership of the North Wales Quarrymen's Union was deeply suspicious of the local leaders in Dinorwig. The union had not called the strike, and there was more than a whiff of betrayal about the way in which the union finally ended it. There were certainly some elements of religious favouritism present in the quarry, and they contributed to the bitterness of the dispute, but the struggle itself arose directly out of issues concerned with the organiza-tion of work and the relations of production and as a reaction to new managerial policies aimed at restricting the men's control of the labour process. The dispute arose directly out of the experience of the quarrymen at their work and the union and its leaders were fairly incidental to the dispute. No union at all was involved in Llanddulas, where the dispute concerned a new contract of employment.

North Wales Quarrymen's Union banner.

Moreover, unrest in the quarrying industry was not a new development which burst upon a previously contented workforce. In the neighbouring Penrhyn Quarries there had been a dispute of some importance as early as 1825 (F.6), more unrest in the 1840s and a serious attempt to form a trade union in 1865. And disputes in the slate quarries often involved mass and threatening tactics as well as walk-outs. In 1877, for example, hundreds of men marched upon, and occupied, a slate quarry in order to drive out Cornishmen working on a new contract system (F.7).

There was also a history of intermittent dispute and conflict, sometimes violent, in the other extractive industries of north Wales. The coal-mining industry of north-east Wales had a long association with trade *unionism*, and an experience of struggle most tragically displayed in the Mold 'riots' of 1869 which had claimed the lives of two colliers and two women shot by the military. But there had been clashes, too, of differing levels of seriousness between other workers and their employers: in Llanddulas itself Fusiliers from Chester had been brought into the village in 1829 to quell rebellious limestone quarrymen who were opposing the enclosure of common land. Strikes were also common in the lead and copper mines of north Wales, particularly in response to employers' attempts to lengthen the hours of work, and change the nature of the wages system: Halkyn miners rioted in 1822 and in 1850 miners armed with sticks won a reduction of hours in Holywell. In 1853 there was a year-long strike in the Llandudno copper mines, but the most dramatic conflict was that of the 500 miners at the Talargoch lead mine in 1856 which witnessed the arrival of the military to counter the attacks of groups of strikers dressed as women, some of whom were carrying, and shooting, firearms (F.8).

The workers of the extractive industries of north Wales, therefore, were not unfamiliar with industrial struggle and the tactics of direct action, tactics which they employed in defence of their working conditions, their wages, or their hours of work.

The early years of the slate industry had been characterized by constant disputations between quarrymen, some of whom were also small cottagers, and landowners, as to access to land being

F.6

F.7

F.8

enclosed either for industrial or agricultural use. These disputes led to a general belief that the mountains had been stolen from the inhabitants and that they still had rights to quarry on land legally owned by others. As late as 1845 we can see this issue leading to a situation in the Cilgwyn district, above the Nantlle Valley in Caernarfonshire, where rival groups of quarrymen contested the right to the produce of the mountains (F.8). This kind of dispute was equally familiar in areas where there was no mineral or other wealth to be guarded; the north Wales countryside had long been accustomed to direct action protests by cottagers, squatters and others.

F.8

Both in industry and in agriculture, therefore, north Wales had a long history of popular disturbance and protest but this is not the picture which was portrayed by the protagonists as they confronted each other before the Royal *Commissioners* of the 1890s. Both sides had their political reasons for not drawing attention to the endemic unrest in the north Wales countryside: the radicals because they did not want to be associated with behaviour which was lawless and opposed to property rights, and which often did not have a clearly defined political target; the landowners because it did not fit their argument about a peaceful countryside disturbed by radicals. Consequently, newpapers, too, were reticent about the subject; it was not the stuff of pamphleteering and the historian often has to consult the records of those responsible for law enforcement to discover the extent, and nature, of the unrest in the north Wales countryside.

Much of the bitterness which existed had to do with the desperately difficult task of making any kind of living on inhospitable heaths and hostile hills and by the desperate desire for more land. But it was a hard life made harder by what were perceived as grievances associated with, although not always caused by, the unequal distribution of land ownership. By the mid-century the hardest hit were the squatters and cottagers who, like the quarrymen of the Cilgwyn, had relied for their livelihoods on access to the open mountain. As land was increasingly enclosed so we find a persistent protest emerging in the countryside. This protest originated in the early years of the century but continued for many decades: in 1855 a number of men were charged that in Llangystennin they did 'riotously and tumultuously assemble and pull down a certain wall or fence', and such behaviour seems to have been repeated in north Wales F.10 for many years (F.10). One of the most notable examples of this species of resistance was the reaction to the enclosure of land in the parish of Caerhun, above Conwy, and neighbouring parishes, in 1858: two thirds of the land went to two landowners and the cottagers, who depended on access to the mountain, got little or nothing and consequently they kept up an intermittent campaign of 'outrages' for ten years. During this time their main tactic was the overthrow during the night of the large stone boundary walls erected during the day. It was a protest which deeply concerned the authorities all the way up to the F.11 Home Office (F.11).

These were protests by the landless in defence of their right to graze their flocks on the mountain, but tenant farmers could also labour under a sense of grievance and bitterness, often because of a sense of insecurity, and a fear that they would not be compensated for improvements which they had made. The political evictions in Merioneth following the election of 1859 had made the names of the farms and farmers persecuted into a popular martyrology although, in truth, the number directly evicted in this ruthless way was small — far more slate quarrymen were to lose their employment for voicing their opinions. But they nevertheless raised a spectre and emphasized the general insecurity of the tenant farmer, whose tenancy could be affected in so many ways: change in ownership of land, the natural disasters of agriculture, changes in rent and in the market. Not many farmers needed to lose their tenancies for all to fear such a loss. One witness to the Royal Commission on Land pathetically related his eviction, with no compensation, when his farm near Tremadoc was bought by one landowner from another; he had subsequently been forced to work as a quarry labourer in Bethesda. Such cases, however rare, caused tension and unrest, often expressed in the vicious language of anonymous letters. Wales, as *Lord Penrhyn* often claimed, seemed to be a land addicted to the sending of such letters, perhaps the most basic of all direct action tactics. One anonymous letter, sent to a new tenant on a farm in north

Merionethshire in 1871, presumably by the displaced tenant, expressed vividly the bitterness and anger which seems to have been the common currency for many living in the countryside
F.12   (F.12). Such a letter would never have appeared in the columns of a newspaper, or as evidence to a commission; it survives, as do so many documents which testify to the hidden but violent passions of the countryside, in the records of the local police. The letter shows that anger was not always directed against the landowner, and that others could also receive anonymous letters — but it also chillingly displays the bitterness of the dispossessed.

As this letter shows, the history of protest and popular action in countryside and quarry should not necessarily be taken as evidence of a people united behind a radical programme. The power and the patronage of landowners and large employers, often the same people, also demanded loyalty and obedience. One should not be surprised to find people behaving in what might appear to us to be a highly contradictory manner and much of the evidence suggests that they did so behave. A propensity to protest could coexist with deference: historians who emphasize the one often exclude the other for the sake of the tidiness of an argument. Such paradoxical behaviour by workers and farmers, could, indeed, be quite rational, as the Penrhyn quarrymen recognized in 1865 when attempting to set up their union: they knew that to antagonize their employer would threaten the union's existence, and despite their pro-testations of loyalty and affection that opposition did indeed
F.13   crush the new arrival (F.13).

Nine years later, in 1874, the *annus mirabilis* of the union, the employers were not successful and the union triumphed by humiliating some of the richest employers in Wales. The new North Wales Quarrymen's Union which emerged in 1874 was to become a major target for the slate masters and the momentous struggles in the slate industry in 1885–6, 1896–7 and 1900–03 were primarily designed to crush that union's power. One of the employers' main complaints was that the union was an 'outside' body interfering with the relationship of master and worker. This charge carried particular force as it appeared to confirm the suspicion that middle-class political

The (Tithe) Martyrs. (*Source: National Library of Wales.*)

agitators were disturbing the social peace. The first officials of the North Wales Quarrymen's Union were, after all, local Welsh businessmen of some substance. In the 1880s, similarly, landowners were conscious of the intervention of *Thomas Gee* and others in the *Tithe War*.

The widespread *Tithe War*, of course, which affected many north Wales counties in the 1880s as farmers refused to pay a '*tithe*' which many saw as oppressive, was perfectly fitted to the political programme of radical liberalism: it directly raised issues of *Nonconformist* rights and Church *Disestablishment* and involved not the landless squatter but the respectable, and therefore more acceptable, farmer. The dramatic direct action tactics of the farmers, particularly during their disruption of *distraining* proceedings, were to be overlooked or forgiven by
F.14   Liberal commentators when placed in this context (F.14).

It is hardly surprising, therefore, that the landowners and their allies considered the disturbances to have been manufactured by their political adversaries but, as we have seen, the unrest can be placed in a long tradition of popular resistance in north Wales and it did, moreover, draw upon a genuine sense of grievance experienced by quarryworkers and rural workers and farmers. This grievance had not been consistently articulated in a programmatic manner and could, on the contrary, express itself in apparently contradictory forms: come the morning the night-time poacher might take his hat off to his landlord. During the 1870s in the slate industry, and the 1880s in the rural economy, the fears and insecurities of a people living in a massively unequal society (and north Wales had a greater concentration of wealth than any other part of England and Wales), were available for the ideologists of the new Wales
F.15   to weave into their political programmes (F.15), a process accelerated by the 'great' depression, in slate from 1878 and in agriculture shortly afterwards. This the orators and pamphleteers did with relish and resounding success: by this token all unrest and all economic disputes became 'political' and the long-active tradition of popular resistance and direct action was recruited into, and subsumed by, a Welsh *Nonconformist* 'world-view'.

The unrest in north Wales can only be understood if we go

beyond the claims of propagandists, but equally we must guard against divorcing the propagandists from their contemporary listeners and supporters. 'Politics' and 'protest' were not diseased bacteria wilfully injected into an otherwise healthy body politic; on the contrary, they, at one and the same time, drew upon, and reacted against, the paradoxes and tensions of the situation. Radical liberalism created a 'common sense' which coexisted with the reflexes of protest which themselves were to continue for many decades: ricks and buildings were still to burn, gates to be left open, rivers poached and crowds of men and women were to continue to gather together noisily to demand redress of their grievances. This alternative 'common sense' affected not only the politics of parliamentary and local elections but it could also be present in the material concerns of economic life, be they rural or industrial. The relationship between this radical 'common sense' and formal politics was not always straightforward, and it could be contradictory, but in late nineteenth-century north Wales the one informed, moulded and fed the other. In the manifesto of the locked-out men of Dinorwig, the language of craft, quarry and *Nonconformist Radicalism* eloquently merge, as it so often did in the north Wales of the 1880s, into a statement which combines grievance with confidence, anger with the determination to achieve change (F.17).

F.17

Sources

F.1   To the Electors of Merionethshire:
Gentlemen,
    I ask for your votes as the chosen candidate of the Liberal Party in Merionethshire.
    Mr Gladstone is ready to listen to the voice and entreaty of Ireland for the right to run her own affairs, by her own sons, on her own land. I give him my warmest support.
    It is time for Parliament to listen to the voice of Wales. It is demanding the *Disestablishment* of the Church of England in

Wales, and the use of its endowments for the good of the nation generally.

It is desirous of perfection in its educational system — the poor like the rich to have the same opportunities to take advantage of all the educational resources of the nation.

It is demanding a thorough reform in the Land Acts, in order to guarantee security of home, fair rents and the security of the fruits of the labourers of the worker, the farmer, and the merchant.

It is demanding Home Rule, so that the control of the drink trade, public appointments, and the means of national development are in the hands of the Welsh people.

From complete conviction I will do what is in me to support these measures and every measure for the improvement of the people of Wales.

> I am, gentlemen,
> Your obedient servant,
> Thomas Edward Ellis.

Cynlas,
Llandderfel,
28 June, 1886.

(National Library of Wales.)

F.2 Major J. M. Clayton, Chief Constable of Caernarvonshire to the Under Secretary of State at the Home Office.

'The men at the quarries are on strike, they and their associates for miles around have banded themselves together to resist the employment of others in the quarries. Endeavours have been made to protect the peace, but without the least success. Rioting of a serious nature has been commenced and staves have been fairly used.'
Dec. 17, 1885.

(Public Records Office, HO 144/162/141864.)

F.3 Little notice has been taken in the capitalist press of the lock-out of 3,000 men at Mr G. Assheton Smith's slate quarry at Llanberris (sic). Naturally enough. A more atrocious case of landlord and capitalist tyranny has rarely been recorded. These

3,000 men were locked out at the beginning of the cold weather in order to force them to accept the owner's terms. Yet this owner has been receiving £150,000 a year or £3,000 a week out of these men's labour for years past. Can we wonder that the men have now combined to drive the manager, Mr Vivian, off the place, and have decided to kill him if he returned? Such 'rights of property' as those enforced by this infamous Smith are an outrage on humanity.

(*Justice*, 19 December 1885.)

F.4   Some of the Welsh landowners are about the best men who ever wore shoes. They are kind and affectionate, and have shown their sympathy with their poor tenants in a substantial way. But it is surprising how few of these there are. It is almost as difficult to get hold of a white rook in Wales, or a white elephant in Bengal, as it is to find a kind landlord. It is necessary for a man to walk scores of miles over hills and vales, through the wilderness and the forests, past many a village and hamlet, before he will see the cheerful face of one of these characters. A kind landlord! He is a lamb amongst wolves, a Liberal amongst *Tories*, a John Howard amongst slaveholders, a kind John amongst bums and scamps. A kind landlord! Let every child lisp his name, every maid sing his praises, every philanthropist declare his praise, and every bard make a crown of roses for him. The common idea of a landlord is a man who has the mouth of a hog, the teeth of a lion, the nails of a bear, the hoofs of an ass, the sting of a serpent, and the greed of the grave. The sailor knows well about the *sharks* of the sea, and the farmers know well the *sharks* of the land. The landowners of our country are, in general, cruel, unreasonable, unfeeling, and unpitying men. It does not matter to them who gets drowned so long as they are allowed to be in the lifeboat; it does not matter to them who suffer the mortal pangs of poverty and hunger, if they have plenty of luxuries. Many of them have been about the most presumptuous thieves that have ever breathed. When a man kills thousands of his fellow men he is called a hero, and his praises are sung by the bells and trumpets of the kingdom, but when he kills one he has the privilege of shaking hands with the hangman and of feeling the rope rather tightly round his neck.

(*Baner ac Amserau Cymru*, 2 November 1887. Trans. in Vincent, p.22.)

F.5   ... the alleged Welsh Land Question is a plant of quite recent growth. Twenty years ago, nay, fifteen years ago, it was unheard of ... It may be asked how it came about that the appearance of a Land Question was brought about in a community having, on the whole, so happy a history ... The answer is to be found in the weighty words addressed to the Commission by *Lord Penrhyn* at Llangefni on the 14th October, 1893 ... but before those words are cited it is necessary to make a few observations ... Between 1880 and 1890 the agitation against the Church was at its height. It took the form, on paper, of the Anti-*tithe* League; it took the form, in practice, of organized resistance to the payment of the *tithe*-rent-charge culminating in riots, some of them of a very serious character, at Mochdre (Flintshire), Meifod (Montgomeryshire), Amlwch and Bodffordd (Anglesey), and spread in an acute form to the counties of Carnarvon, Cardigan and Merioneth. In fact the Welsh people, who are by nature as quiet and peaceloving a people as any in the world, were, during the decade mentioned, in a state nearer to general lawlessness ... than during any other period of the century ... it is certain that until the anti-*tithe* agitation in Wales became acute, nothing whatsoever was heard about a Welsh Land Question ... Hence came it that *Lord Penrhyn* addressed to the Commission [the Royal Commission on Land of 1896] the words (Q.2279 and onwards) to which reference has been made. Speaking as the Chairman of a body of landowners practically representing the whole of North Wales ... he said, 'I next desire to lay before the Commission, in the most earnest manner and as being vital to the whole question, facts which, in my opinion, prove that the agitation upon the Welsh Land Question was unreal in origin, and had not its source in any genuine sense of grievance on the part of the agricultural community.

(J.E. Vincent, *The Land Question in North Wales*, 1896, pp.5–10.)

179

Threshing at Star, Gaerwen. *(Source: Gwynedd Archives Service.)*

F.6   To The
                        QUARRY MEN
                   AND OTHER WORKERS
                  Of the Penrhyn Slate Quarries
                  Called 'Cae Braich y Cefn'.

NOTICE IS HEREBY GIVEN

To all Quarrymen and other Workmen who are unwilling, and
do not like to return to their Work, that such work will be
immediately measured up and paid off; and all such Persons are
requested forthwith to attend at the Quarry for that purpose.

And all Quarrymen and other Workmen who are desirous and
willing to work, at the said Quarries, on the same terms as
heretofore, are requested immediately to attend their several
employments.

As soon as the Men have returned to their work Mr Wyatt will
enquire into the complaints that have been made, and whatever
appears fair and reasonable, will be redressed:–

Until this is done nothing further can be said.

Penrhyn Castle, 22 March 1825.

(*North Wales Gazette and Weekly Advertiser for the Principality*,
                                    Thursday, 24 March 1825.)

F.7   About four o'clock on Thursday afternoon the inhabitants of
         Bettws Garmon were surprised to see hundreds of quarrymen
         briskly making their way down the mountain sides from the
         direction of Cefn Du Quarry on the one hand, and hundreds
         also descending the mountain slopes opposite from the Nantlle
         side. The latter party stopped above Hafodywern Quarry, and
         the other gang remained on the opposite hill-side. In a short
         time afterwards a number of men from the Cefn Du party were
         seen approaching across the valley to meet the Nantlle
         men, after which they both proceeded in the direction on
         Hafodywern. Their errand may be stated in a few words. The
         proprietors of this quarry had seen fit to frame certain rules for
         their workmen, thereby fixing a different system of hours and

wages from that existing in other neighbourhoods. Of course, the men were displeased with this new arrangement, which was also disagreeable to the other quarrymen working in the neighbourhood.

Angry feelings, of course, were the natural consequences of this belief. The representatives from both gangs of quarrymen visited Hafodywern Quarry with, as they say, peaceful intentions. They endeavoured to reason with the authorities there in reference to the newcomers who were working on terms so totally different from those customary in the neighbourhood. But the authorities in question refused to hear the representatives, who then departed with the answer. After a consultation with the parties standing on both sides of the valley, it was agreed to visit the quarry in a body, and protest against the course adopted. A peculiar whistle was the signal for the start, and all the party, as one man, about eight or nine hundred, began to descend along the mountain sides, and walked to the quarry. On reaching it, the leaders expressed a desire to speak to the workmen, whom they requested to come out for that purpose.

(*Caernarvon and Denbigh Herald,* May 1876.)

F.8   The late disastrous Strike commenced in the beginning of July last and continued for about four months. The immediate cause of the strike was the proposed introduction by the masters of certain new regulations . . .

For several weeks after the commencement of the Strike, the men used to meet every day at the Talargoch Works, to discuss what they considered their grievances. No miner was allowed to absent himself from these meetings, without giving a satisfactory reason. During these weeks the miners conducted themselves very quietly; and it ought to be borne in mind that *before* the Engine was stopped — *before* any act of violence was committed, they expressed their willingness to submit the matter in dispute to arbitration, and to abide by the decision of the Magistrates of the District, or that of any other competent person. A good opportunity of settling the matter in dispute was now lost.

The first act of violence, which was committed in the neighbourhood during the continuance of the Strike, was the pulling down at night of a fence, at Tywyn, in the Parish of Dyserth, enclosing a part of the common, adjoining the property of E. Williamson, Esq., of Holywell. Whether this was done by some of the miners, or by some other persons interested in the preservation of the common, it would be difficult to determine. The same remark may be made respecting the wall, which was thrown down during the night a few days afterwards . . .

The next act of violence was the surrounding of Dyserth Hall, the residence of the late Agent, Mr Ishmael Jones, by some twenty or thirty persons, some of whom were dressed in women's clothes, and carried firearms, which they fired. The inmates, of course, were much alarmed, but no one was hurt, and no damage was done to anything about the house. The same party is supposed to have visited the Talargoch Works. All this took place on the Friday night before the Stopping of the Engines. On the following morning, one or two anonymous letters, supposed to have been addressed to the Engine Drivers (for they were clumsily written) were found near the Works. In consequence of receiving these letters the Engine Drivers became frightened and ceased working the Engines on Saturday, the 2nd August, and about the month after the commencement of the Strike . . .

About the middle of October, the Engines commenced pumping the water again. Two strangers had been engaged to manage them, the old Engine Drivers having been dismissed. The introduction of these strangers, was not at all liked by the miners generally, as it was an understood agreement amongst them, that they were not to return to their work, unless they all returned together.

For some days after the arrival of the new Engine Drivers, and the new Agent, matters went on quietly, but it was a short calm. On the 21st October last, between 10 and 11 o'clock at night, a number of men, supposed to have been 30 or thereabout, went in a body to the Talargoch Works; and some small shot were fired into the Engine-House, where one of the new Engine Drivers was at the time; but fortunately he escaped without being at all hurt. The watchman, Edward Thomas, was also fired at by one of the crowd, and several small shot entered his feet and legs. The room, where the new Agent used to sleep, was also fired into; and so was a room upstairs fired into in the House where the new Engine Drivers lodged. But, most providentially, no one was injured at all, with the exception of Edward Thomas, and he is now almost recovered and talks of returning to his work . . . A reward of £200 has been offered for such information, as would lead to the discovery and conviction of the party guilty of firing at the watchman, together with Her Majesty's pardon to any accomplice, not being a person who actually fired, who should give such evidence as would lead to a like result. Hitherto, however, no evidence has been given respecting the man who wounded Edward Thomas.

It was now felt by the miners and the public generally that after the wounding of the Watchman the Strike was at an end. The Magistrates met on Wednesday, the 22nd of October, and decided upon having a company of soldiers from Chester. The military, about 30 in number, remained at Talgarth for a week, without meeting with the least opposition on the part of the miners, and then returned to Chester; but before their departure, the miners had consented to resume their work upon the terms offered by the masters which were similar to those offered at the commencement of the Strike with the exception that many new regulations were added.

('A Strike at Talargoch Lead-Mine One Hundred Years Ago', written by the Incumbent to the Bishop. National Library of Wales MS. SA/Misc./364.)

F.9   *CILGWYN QUARRIES* — these quarries the property of the late Mr Muskett, MP, have within the last few months been taken possession of by different parties of quarrymen and labourers, who appropriate the produce to their own use, and act upon the principle that 'Might is Right'. Not longer since than last Carnarvon fair-day, a party, who had been fortunate enough to meet with a good piece of rock, and were regaling themselves at the fair, had their ground invaded by a stronger party, who have since kept possession, and obliged the first settlers to content themselves with a less productive spot. A ready sale is found at Carnarvon at reduced prices, and all take care to cart away and dispose with their slates as quickly as possible. There are now, within a trifle, one hundred men at work, and almost every day adds to their number.

(*Caernarvon and Denbigh Herald*, 22 March 1845.)

F.10   THE CONDITION of the within written Recognizance is such, that whereas it hath been duly certified by Richard Anthony Poole Clerk of the Peace of and for the within mentioned County that at a Court of General Quarter Sessions of the peace holden in and for the said County on Thursday the Eighteenth day of October 1855 a Bill of Indictment was found against Patrick Evans, Jem Jones, Robert Jones, Hugh Jones, Robert Davies, Elias Davies, Jesse Davies, and William Roberts for that they did riotously and tumultuously assemble and pull down a certain wall or fence belonging to and in the possession of Jane Rees and did commit other misdemeanours in the said Indictment set forth and that they the above named had not nor had any or either of them appeared or pleaded to the said Indictment. If therefore the above named William Roberts will appear at the next Court of General Quarter Sessions of the Peace to be holden at Caernarvon in and for the County of Caernarvon, and there surrender himself into the custody of the Keeper of the Common Gaol there, and plead to the said Indictment, for or in respect of the charge aforesaid, and take his trial upon the same, and not depart the said Court without leave, then the said Recognizance to be void, or else to stand in full force and virtue.

(Gwynedd Record Office XQS/1856/H/6, Quarter Session Records.)

F.11   In the Parish of Caerhun there were very extensive commons, and that, though right of possession was enjoyed, it was necessary according to an Act of Parliament that a wall should be built enclosing such possessions, before an action for trespass could be enforced. It had now become habitual in that district to pull down the walls, and it was not unusual for a man possessing scarcely more than a cottage to have 400 or 600 sheep grazing on the commons. It was also stated that a great many petitions had been received in opposition to the forming of the contemplated extra police district . . . Sir Richard [*Bulkeley*] thought these acts would not be committed in the day time, and that therefore the services of policemen would not be of any avail . . . Sir Richard said there was an opinion among the lower orders that they had a right to the commons as long as they were unenclosed. The Chairman thought the government would refuse the annual grant unless this new district was formed or something done to curb the lawlessness of that district. The Chief Constable, in answer to the question as what additions to the force he would require to look after this district, said he should require to begin at least twenty additional men. Many thought that double or treble that number would not suffice. Mr R.D. Williams . . . thought many of the tenants of Sir Richard and other gentlemen on the bench were implicated.

(*Caernarvon and Denbigh Herald*, 6 July 1867. Caernarfonshire Quarter Sessions.)

F.12 . . . Heddyw yr ydych yn gorfod ymostwng i'ch meistr tir — cyn pen ychydig ddyddiau eto bydd raid i chwi ymostwng i un uwch na hwnw, wylo yr oeddych am gael tir Dolmoch, os ydych am gael marw yn fuan aroswch ar y tir tynghadof chwi trwy hun os ewch i fyw ir lle ydych wedi ei gymeryd mai byr amser fydd genych i fyw, ac y byddwch marw y truenaf o blant dynion nid ar y tir yr ydych yn dymuno marw arno, ond lle nas gallant gael hyd i'ch corff nes y bydd ehediaid yr awyr wedi bwyta rhan ohono fel y byddo digon o farn y Duw goruchaf arnoch yn y byd hwn, am eith castiau drygionus, a chymeryd y farn yn y byd a ddaw heb law hun yna.

(Today you have to submit to your landlord — before very many more days you will have to submit to someone higher than him, you wept to get the land of Dolmoch, if you want to die soon stay on that land, I promise you through this that if you go to live to the place you have taken then you will only have a short while to live, and that you will die the most pitiful of the children of men not on the land that you wish to die on, but a place where they will not be able to find your body until the larks of the air will have eaten parts of it so that there will be enough of the judgement of God above on you while you are in this world, for your evil doings, and you will still have to take the judgement to come in addition to that here.)

(Gwynedd Record Office. Police Letter Book (Merioneth). 28 February 1871.)

F.13   Bore Sadwrn diweddaf rhwng 1200 a 1500 yn Mynydd y Cefn . . . Robert Thomas, ysgrifennydd yr Undeb — Cymdeithas Undebol Chwarelwyr Cymru i ymdrechu coethi chwaeth a dyrchafu y chwarelwyr fel dosbarth o grefftwyr yn y gymdeithas ddynol . . . ceisio ymdrechu hyd eithaf eu gallu i fynu gwaith i'r meistr a chyflog priodol i'r gweithiwr (a fair day's wages for a fair day's work) . . . nid ein hamcan ydyw ymosod ar neb, na chyfodi gwrthryfel yn erbyn neb . . . nid diffyg ymddiried yn ein meistr . . . ydyw achos ein bod yn ceisio sefydlu Union . . . Robert Thomas a Robert Parry yn cynig 'Ein bod ni fel chwarelwyr yn datgan ein hymddiried llwyraf yn anrhydedd a gair ein meistr yr Anrhydeddus Filwriad Pennant, ac yn ei gudnabod yn ddiolchgar am ei ymddygiad caredig tuag atom pan yn trafod y pwnc gydag ef.' Rhoddwyd tair banllef iawn iddo, nes oedd yr asdain trwy yr holl fynnydd.

(Last Saturday morning between 1,200 and 1,500 gathered on Mynydd y Cefn . . . Robert Thomas, the Union Secretary, said that *Cymdeithas Undebol Chwarelwyr Cymru* (The United Society of Welsh Quarrymen) would attempt to refine taste and raise the quarrymen as a class of craftsmen in human society . . . would seek to the utmost to secure work for the master and appropriate wages for the worker (a fair day's wages for a fair day's work) . . . our aim is not to attack anybody nor raise rebellion against anybody . . . it is not lack of trust in our master . . . which is the reason for trying to establish a Union . . . Robert Thomas and Robert Parry proposed that 'We as quarrymen express our complete confidence in the honour and the word of our master the Hon. *Colonel Pennant*, and we recognize gratefully his kind behaviour towards us when we discussed matters with him.' Three real shouts were given until the noise echoed throughout the whole mountain . . . 1,543 from Chwarel y Cae have joined the union.)

(*Yr Herald Cymraeg*, 11 November 1865.)

F.14   A number of Cwm Eithin farmers resolved not to pay *tithe* at all unless a reduction was granted. The result was that on the eighteenth of May, 1887, the Ecclesiastical *Commissioners* decided to *distrain* on the goods of about eighty farmers who had refused to pay. The alarm was sounded, crowds gathered at the threatened farms and in many cases it was found impossible to seize the goods. In three farms, however, goods were *distrained* upon. This meant that a sale was to follow, and on June 1, 1887, there was a forced sale of two cows at Fron Isa, where my cousin and her husband, Thomas Hughes, lived.

By six o'clock on the morning of that day twenty five members of the Denbighshire constabulary, with an inspector, had arrived at Fron Isa, but the auctioneer and his assistants were late, and by the time they arrived all the people of the district were there also — every farmer with his stout stick and the farm servants with cudgels, while the womenfolk encouraged them to give battle to the authorities. The auctioneer put the cows up for sale, but not a penny was bid and the attitude of the crowd was threatening. As there were no bids for the cattle an attempt was made to remove them but the crowd refused to allow this to be done; the two cows were worth four times the amount of *tithe* due from the farmer. In the circumstances the auctioneer and his companions were glad to get away with unbroken bones. I have heard that they and their police protectors were escorted by some three hundred people along the road past Y Glyn in the Corwen direction. It was an angry and to all appearance a threatening crowd.

It was understood that there were to be sales at other farms but the direction from which the auctioneers and their followers would come was doubtful. It was decided to set a watch, and it was then that what we may call the first telephonic communication was installed in Cwm Eithin. Watchers were posted on a number of selected heights, each man being near enough to the next sentinel to be able to make himself heard by him, and it was arranged that a number of beacons should be lit as soon as the auctioneer's cavalcade was sighted. Horsemen were in readiness to raise the alarm through the countryside as soon as the news of the enemy's approach was received. The auctioneer eventually came from the Cerrig y Drudion direction, driving in a carriage and pair, and the warning went round at once. By the time he arrived at the farm where the forced sale was to be held a great crowd was already there waiting for him. The carriage was stopped and the auctioneer and his men ordered to come out and told to walk away in the Corwen direction. The driver was allowed to remain on the box but the horses were frightened and bolted.

There was nothing the auctioneer's party could do but obey; they started to walk towards Corwen and when they were passing the deep pool in the river by Y Glyn someone suggested that the auctioneer should be thrown in, and had the leaders of the revolt not interposed it is quite possible that violence might have been used. As it was, the 'invaders' were convinced that they were in serious peril and begged for their lives. They were told to kneel on the road and presented with the following declaration which they signed:

> 'We hereby promise not to come on this business again in any part of England or Wales to sell for Tithes.'

They were then made to take off their coats and to put them on wrong side out, to show their repentance. After that a procession to escort them to Corwen railway station, a distance of five miles, was arranged — the representatives of the Church in the middle, with their coats the wrong side out, a red flag before and a black flag behind, with a shouting and screaming crowd all around them.

(Hugh Evans, *The Gorse Glen*, Trans., 1948.)

F.15 LANDOWNERS OF CAERNARFONSHIRE AND DENBIGHSHIRE

CAERNARFON			DENBIGH		
No. of Owners	Class.	Acres	No. of Owners	Class.	Acres
4	Peers	102,470	0	Peers	20,812
10	Great Landowners	100,861	16	Great Landowners	130,165
*19	Squires	32,300	†38	Squires	64,600
42	Greater Yeomen	21,000	106	Greater Yeomen	53,000
96	Lesser Yeomen	16,320	254	Lesser Yeomen	43,180
1,407	Small Proprietors	23,527	1,773	Small Proprietors	31,436
4,610	Cottagers	373	3,436	Cottagers	721
52	Public Bodies	4,382	85	Public Bodies	4,503
	Waste	14,563		Waste	18,812
6,240	—Total	315,796	5,708	—Total	367,229

* Only six of these have over £1,000 rental.

† Sixteen of these have less than £1,000 per annum.

(John Bateman, *Great Landowners of Great Britain* (1876, 1883).)

F.16 The real cause of the ill feeling among the men at both Llanberis and Llanddulas is political. There is no doubt of it . . .

(18 December 1885. Chairman of Caernarvonshire Quarter Sessions to Home Office. Public Record Office. HO 144/162/A4 1864.)

F.17 In the foregoing account we have touched upon the principal facts in the history of this case to enable the public to judge for itself as to the behaviour of the men and the action of the managers. We do not want to pass judgment upon them, this we leave to the public and the press of the country, which always gives its helping hand to those who are oppressed or harshly and unjustly treated. We do not want to justify every action taken by us. We may have erred in small matters, but we cannot bring ourselves to believe that the treatment we are receiving is in any sense justified by these small mistakes. We may be wrong, but we do believe that religious and political questions have more to do with it than appears on the surface. We are expected to be more pliable — not simply workmen and obedient servants — but servile vassals. We have been told that we are too independent. The charge has not been made against us that we are not good workmen. The distribution of favours for religious and political services goes a long way to prove that no high price is put at the Dinorwic Quarries for manly independence, honesty, faithfulness to work, and good workmanship. That which should elevate a workman, and pays the employer best, is at a discount; and that which degrades him is covered with favour, and receives as a reward that which should only be given to the best and most honourable of the class.

We highly respect our employer, and should have been glad to be able to rejoice in the two principal managers. They may try and crush us, but they will fail. We shall throw ourselves upon the charity of the public, and even upon the *poor rates*, however degrading that may be to us, before we shall start on the road that leads to slavery. It is more honourable to be poor and the recipients of charity than degraded servile vassals. The character of a slave owner is not an exalted one, though he is constituted one by others (and we feel sure that our late employer would be the last to wish to see us so degraded): and the character of slave driver has for ever been given its proper status by *Uncle Tom's Cabin*. Nothing that we can say can add to the repulsiveness of such a character.

Having been thrown upon the world by the cruel treatment of unfeeling men; and having to provide for ourselves and our dear ones in the winter that is now upon us, we appeal for help to all mankind, and especially to all our countrymen all over the world, to assist us to prevent the best class of Welsh workmen being trodden upon as mere slaves.

T. Closs Williams	William Hughes
Griffith Griffiths	W. Parry Jones
Francis W. Francis	J. Foulkes
William R. Jones	J. Jones

14th Dec. 1885

(*The Lock-Out at Dinorwic Quarries*, Caernarfon, 1885, published by the Lock-Out Committee.)

Debating the evidence

We return to the theme of social protest in Dr Merfyn Jones's essay, although we now focus our attention on north Wales. The range of sources used by Dr Jones is mostly of the type already commented upon. Some are English translations of material originally written in Welsh. Remembering that historians should always attempt to understand historical evidence as it was conveyed and understood at the time, might translation pose problems? Quarter Sessions records provide the first examples of legal records we have encountered. Are they factual, objective documents of record or must they be subjected to critical analysis? Merfyn Jones also shows clearly how examples of subjective evidence can be tellingly juxtaposed Alongside *Thomas Gee*, the prominent *Nonconformist* and radical publisher who through his Welsh Land League led the fight against landlordism, we have J. E. Vincent, a barrister employed by the North Wales Property Defence League to fight the corner of the landowners. Here is polemic at its height.

Source F.1
For what is this primary evidence? What does this source tell us about the influence of *Nonconformity* on *T. E. Ellis?*

Source F.2
To what is the Chief Constable referring in the first sentence here? Why would this report have been sent to the Home Office?

Source F.3
What words in this report indicate bias in this newspaper? What are the strengths of this source?

Source F.4
How does this source compare with F.3?

Source F.5
What do you make of the author's claim that the Welsh people were 'by nature as quiet and peaceloving a people as any in the world'? Remembering what you know about their authors, compare this source with source F.4 — how do you assess their reliability as evidence on the 'Land Question'?

Source F.6
Why would it be important to establish the precise meaning of 'measured up and paid off'? Why do you think the Quarry Owners had this published?

Source F.7
What questions might you ask about the reliability of this source as evidence for what happened at Hafodywern Quarry in May 1876?

Source F.8
How does the authorship of this source affect your view of its reliability as evidence? What is the significance of the reference to some of the persons who attacked Dyserth Hall being 'men dressed in women's clothes'? Does this indicate that they were similar incidents to the *Scotch Cattle* and Rebecca?

Source F.9
How might part of the evidence in Source F.8 be seen to support the point Dr Jones is illustrating in this source?

Source F.10
What difficulties are there in using evidence from this source? Why did the accused pull down Jane Rees's wall or fence? Why does the latter part of this document refer only to William Roberts?

Source F.11
What evidence is there here which helps us assess popular attitudes to the types of action mentioned in this source and in Source F.10? Compare the evidence here to the claims made in Source F.8.

Source F.12
What significance does Dr Jones believe such letters have, despite their anonymity?

Source F.13
Why, in assessing its reliability, is it important to discover how this source was created? What in Merfyn Jones's essay might cast doubt on some of the evidence here?

Source F.14

What indications are there here that the author of this source was involved in the events described? On this basis what do you see as being the strengths and weaknesses of this evidence?

Source F.15

How might the evidence here have been collected? What does it show about land ownership in north Wales at this time?

Source F.16

Why might you question this statement?

Source F.17

In assessing the views of quarrymen in north Wales at this time, compare the value of this source to that of Sources F.9 and F.13. On what basis — mentioned by Dr Jones — might you be sceptical of some of the evidence here?

Discussion

Dr Merfyn Jones's essay provides an example of how an historian uses evidence to re-interpret historical stereotypes. His critique is directed as much towards the views of the influential *Thomas Gee* and the tradition he represents (Sources F.1, F.4) as it is to the pro-landlord position of J. E. Vincent (Source F.5). Jones uses evidence such as Sources F.2, F.7 and F.8 to challenge the view of Welsh history in the nineteenth century developed by *Nonconformists* and Radicals. In illustrating the longevity in north Wales of protest against social and economic conditions, he identifies, broadly, developments taking place there with those considered by David Jones and David Howell in south Wales. In seeking direct evidence from working people in north Wales, Merfyn Jones is faced by the same problems we have noted earlier. Probably because north Wales was far less industrialized than the south there was not the degree of official enquiries and investigation which furnished material for earlier essays. Newspaper sources do exist (Sources F.3, F.6, F.7, F.13, etc.), but again their obvious bias is a limiting factor in assessing the extent to which they reflected the views of ordinary people. This, as Merfyn Jones points out, is why a source such as F.17, with all its obvious limitations, is potentially so valuable. The records of trade unions and other working-class organizations (Source F.17) must be treated with circumspection but at least they allow a rare glimpse into working-class opinion, expressed through its leadership. With all its attendant problems, anonymous material (such as F.12) enables us to encounter directly searing discontent and frustration. In all such cases, of course, it is the historian's interpretation which is crucial. Merfyn Jones would be the first to recognize that his sources would also be used by the historian stressing more traditional or alternative interpretations.

Further Reading

Ashton, O., 'Chartism in Mid-Wales', *The Montgomeryshire Collections*, 62, 1, 1971.

Bassett, T.M., *The Welsh Baptists*, Swansea, 1977.

Carter, H., *The Towns of Wales*, Cardiff, 1966.

Carter, H. and Wheatley, S., *Merthyr Tydfil in 1851. A Study of the Spatial Structure of a Welsh Industrial Town*, Cardiff, 1982.

Carter, H. and Wheatley, S., 'Transformations in the spatial structure of Welsh towns in the nineteenth century' in *Transactions of the Honourable Society of Cymmrodorion*, 1980

Daunton, M.J., *Coal Metropolis*, Leicester, 1977.

Davies, E.T., *Religion in the Industrial Revolution in South Wales*, Cardiff, 1959.

Davies, E.T., *Religion and Society in the Nineteenth Century*, Llandybïe, 1981.

Dodd, A.H., *The Industrial Revolution in North Wales*, second edition, Cardiff, 1951.

Dunbabin, J.P.D., *Rural Discontent in Nineteenth-Century Britain*, London, 1974.

Howell, D., *Land and People in Nineteenth Century Wales*, London, 1978.

John, A., 'The Chartist Endurance: Industrial South Wales, 1840–68', *Morgannwg*, XV, 1971.

Jones, D.J.V., *Before Rebecca: Popular Protest in Wales 1793–1835*, London, 1973.

Jones, D.J.V., *The Last Rising. The Newport Insurrection of 1839*, Oxford, 1985.

Jones, I.G., *Explorations and Explanations. Essays in the Social History of Victorian Wales*, Llandysul, 1981.

Jones, I.G., *Health, Wealth and Politics in Victorian Wales*, Swansea, 1979.

Jones, R. Merfyn, *The North Wales Quarrymen 1874–1922*, Cardiff, 1981.

Jones, R. Merfyn, 'Notes from the Margin: Class and Society in Nineteenth Century Gwynedd', in D. Smith, ed., *A People and a Proletariat*, London, 1980.

Jones, R. Tudur, *Hanes Annibynwyr Cymru*, Abertawe, 1966.

Lambert, W.R., *Drink and Sobriety in Victorian Wales*, Cardiff, 1983.

Lindsay, Jean, *A History of the North Wales Slate Industry*, Newton Abbot, 1974.

Molloy, P., *And They Blessed Rebecca*, Llandysul, 1983.

Morgan, K.O., *Wales in British Politics 1868–1922*, revised edition, Cardiff, 1970.

Smith, D., ed., *A People and a Proletariat*, London, 1980.

Wilks, I., *South Wales and the Rising of 1839*, London, 1984.

Williams, D., *John Frost: A Study in Chartism*, Cardiff, 1939.

Williams, D., *The Rebecca Riots: A Study in Agrarian Discontent*, Cardiff, 1955.

Glossary

Acts of Union The name given to a series of Acts of Parliament passed between 1536 and 1543 which united Wales with England.

Anti-Corn Law League An alliance of people opposed to the Corn Laws (Cobden was one of the most important). These Corn Laws kept up the price of corn against foreign competition. In 1815 foreign imports of corn were forbidden unless the home price was above 80*s*. a quarter. Repeal of the Corn Laws in 1846 split the Tory Party and resulted in *Peel*'s resignation.

Baptist Nonconformist religious denomination, practising baptism by total immersion in water.

Benthamite One who believes in the views of Jeremy Bentham, the eminent utilitarian, that is someone who believed in policies (and a morality) which would result in the greatest good of the greatest number.

Blackleg Person who works in defiance of a trade union when there is a strike.

Blue Books of 1847 The published findings of a Government enquiry into the state of education in Wales in 1846–7. Profoundly condemnatory of education and most things Welsh.

Bourgeoisie The middle class or entrepeneurial, owning, capitalist class created by the Industrial Revolution.

Bulkeley The major landowning family in Anglesey with origins going back beyond the Tudor period.

Bute Estate	A vast landed estated belonging to the nineteenth-century Marquises of Bute, centred on Cardiff Castle, located in Glamorgan, though the Butes had extensive lands in England and Scotland too. The Butes made fortunes from royalties on coal dug from under their land.
Calvinistic Methodist	See *Methodist*.
Captain Swing	— also referred to as the Swing riots. These were rick-burning episodes in southern England, from Kent to Dorset, in 1830. They took place at night against a background of increasing agrarian and industrial unrest in grim economic conditions. Suppressed by Home Secretary, Lord Melbourne, with great harshness. Nine hanged, 1,000 transported.
Cardis	People who came from the former county of Cardiganshire.
Ceffyl Pren	— literally 'wooden horse'. A means by which the community imposed its moral code — effigies of offenders (for example, adulterers) were placed on a ladder and paraded around the streets. Particularly prevalent in south-west Wales.
Chartism	A mainly working-class movement aimed at extending the vote and reforming Parliament. Worked for the People's Charter (hence the name) after 1838, demanding universal suffrage, annual Parliaments, secret ballot, payment of members of Parliament, equal electoral districts and the abolition of the property qualification for MPs.
Chartist Rising	The three-pronged Chartist march on Newport in 1839 which ended in tragedy as marchers were fired upon by soldiers stationed in the Westgate Hotel, Newport.
Church Rates	Taxes which went towards the upkeep of the established Church, therefore incensing Nonconformist Wales. Attempts at abolition were channelled into

Parliament. There were unsuccessful abolition bills in 1837, 1861 and 1867.

Combinations	Early name for trade unions.
Commissioners	People appointed by the Government to conduct Parliamentary investigation, e.g. the Poor Law Commission in 1832.
Company Shops	Also known as Truck Shops, i.e. shops run by employing companies, for example, ironworks, where workers could redeem the tokens in which they had been paid. This system was open to abuse by the owners.
Corn Law	See *Anti-Corn Law League.*
Cyfarthfa	One of the four great Merthyr ironworks — established in 1780. Its most famous (or infamous) owners, the Crawshay dynasty of ironmasters.
Disestablishment	The act of separating the Church in Wales from the Church of England which was the established Church, that is the state Church in Wales as well as England until 1920.
Distrain	Taking goods and household possessions away by force from people who would not or could not pay fines in money. Particularly associated with refusal to pay tithes in north Wales in the 1880s and 1890s.
Dorchester Affair	In March 1834 six Dorchester labourers were sentenced to seven years' transportation to a penal colony in Australia for organizing trade union activities in the Dorsetshire village of Tolpuddle. Great public demonstrations resulted eventually in the remittance of the sentences.
Dowlais	One of the four great ironworks in the Merthyr area, owned by the Guest family.
Eisteddfod	A cultural festival, predominantly of poetry and music in the Welsh language. Held locally and nationally, the eisteddfodau have roots in medieval times.

Ellis, T.E.	Thomas Edward Ellis, son of a tenant farmer of Bala, who became chief whip in the Liberal Government before his premature death in 1896. Leader of the *Cymru Fydd* movement for Welsh Home Rule.
Ellis, Tom	See *T.E. Ellis.*
Established Church	See *Disestablishment.*
Feargus O'Connor's Land Plan	Feargus O'Connor was a leading Chartist, who founded the Chartist newspaper, *The Northern Star* in 1837, and advocated the peasant ownership of land.
Friendly Societies	Associations of workers who combined mainly for the purpose of providing insurance benefits of various kinds as opposed to being involved in overtly political action.
Gee, Thomas	Denbigh publisher and preacher who, through his publications, became the leader of political Nonconformity in north Wales. Influential in promoting public opinion against the landowners in the 1868 election.
Gnoll Estate	One of the main landed estates in Neath, West Glamorgan.
Independent	The name given historically to chapels of the Congregationalist denomination and still used for Welsh-language Congregationalist chapels. They were noted for democratic chapel government.
Irish Coercion Bill	Projected legislation of 1880, passed in 1881, to restore order in Ireland after the Irish National Land League had organized tenants into resisting eviction from their land. The first legislation for which the Parliamentary device of the closure was imposed by the Speaker of the House of Commons.
Laissez-Faire	Literally 'let be' or 'leave alone'. This policy is particularly associated with governments of the first half of the nineteenth century who endorsed an

economic and social policy of interfering as little as possible in economic and social matters.

Local Boards of Health	See *Public Health Acts*.
Methodist	Nonconformist denomination particularly strong in north Wales. While in England most Methodists were Wesleyan, so-called after John Wesley, Welsh Methodism generally embraced, at least in theory, the harsh doctrines of John Calvin, the sixteenth-century Protestant reformer, hence Calvinistic Methodists.
Napoleonic Wars	1803–15. In essence a continuation of Britain's involvement in continental wars starting in 1793 when French revolutionary armies had occupied Belgium and France declared war on Britain and Holland. Ended with a final defeat of the Emperor Napoleon at the Battle of Waterloo in 1815.
National Reform League	See *Reform League*.
National Reform Union	See *Reform League*.
New Poor Law	See *Poor Law*.
Newport Rising	See *Chartist Rising*.
Nonconformity	Generic name given to various denominations, mainly Methodist, Baptists and Independents, which had broken away from the established Church, the Church of England.
Northern Star	Best known of the Chartist newspapers. See *Chartism*.
Parry, W.J.	Secretary and one of the leading figures of the North Wales Quarrymen's Union which figured centrally in the dispute with the slate quarry owners from 1874 when it was founded. A Welsh-speaking Liberal Nonconformist who believed in harmony in industrial relations.

Peace Society   As its name implies, a society dedicated to bringing influences to bear on the electorate for policies of peaceful coexistence. The secretary at one time was *Henry Richard*.

Peel, Sir Robert   Prime Minister for two terms between 1834 and 1846. Repealed the *Corn Laws* (see *Anti-Corn Law League*) in 1846, so splitting the Tory Party.

Pennant, Colonel   The owner of one of the largest slate quarries in the world in the second half of the nineteenth century, the Penrhyn quarry. Became Lord Penrhyn in 1866.

Penrhyn, Lord   See *Pennant*.

Penydarren/
Pen-y-daran   One of the four great Merthyr ironworks — started by the Homfray family in the 1780s.

People's Charter   See *Chartism* and *Working Men's Association*.

Plasau/Plastai   The Welsh words for 'gentry houses'.

Plymouth Works   One of the four great Merthyr ironworks along with *Cyfarthfa*, *Dowlais* and *Penydarren*. So called because it was established on land belonging to the Earl of Plymouth.

Poor Law   The system of helping the poor had hardly changed since Tudor times, but was under increasing strain in the early nineteenth century as the poor rate increased for the wealthier members of society. The result was a Poor Law Commission and a *Poor Law Amendment Act* in 1834 which recommended stopping outdoor assistance to the poor and advocated the building of workhouses by parish unions where people would be kept in a condition worse than that of the lowest-paid workers outside.

Proletariat   The working class. Marxists used the word in contradistinction to the *bourgeoisie* or capitalist/middle class.

Public Health
Acts   There were two major public health acts. The first in 1848 resulted from pressure by Chadwick and other

public health reformers to do something to stop the spread of disease, particularly cholera. It created the General Board of Health which could set up *Local Boards of Health* if a) ratepayers petitioned for it, b) the death rate was particularly high. The second act in 1875 was passed by Disraeli and consolidated the 1866 Sanitary Act and other sanitary legislation.

Quakers   A religious sect founded in the seventeenth century characterized by a unique form of service of worship which took no set form. Also known as the Society of Friends. One of the most persecuted of sects because they refused to defer to their 'social superiors'. Known in the nineteenth century for enlightened treatment of workers in factories they owned.

Radicalism   In a nineteenth century context usually refers to the reforming wing of the Liberal Party.

Reform and   Known as the Third Reform Act. The previous
Redistribution   Reform Act in 1867 had given householders and
Act of 1884   lodgers in boroughs the vote; the 1884 Act extended this vote to the counties. There were seven ways by which a person could qualify for the vote, but 80 per cent of voters came under the household and occupation franchise.

Reform League   Formed 1864. Mainly working-class movement campaigning for the vote for all men and for the secret ballot. Strongly supported the Liberals in the 1868 election.

Religious Census   Held in 1851. The only official systematic count of religious worship in modern times — part of the official (decennial) census of 1851. Recorded every person attending morning, afternoon and evening services in places of worship in England and Wales.

Richard, Henry   Independent minister who became secretary of the *Peace Society*, won a famous victory in the 1868 Merthyr election as a Liberal Nonconformist. Then known as 'the member for Wales'.

Scotch Cattle	Secret societies of colliers mainly in Monmouthshire in the 1820s and 1830s who enforced community sanctions against *blacklegs* and profiteers by direct action. The colliers wore masks and cattle skins and were led by a man rigged out with a horned bull's head.
Scotch Law	See *Scotch Cattle*.
Suffrage	The right to vote in parliamentary elections.
Sunday School	Schools held by the religious denominations on Sundays as part of worship. Taught reading from the Bible and, in Wales, embraced adults as well as children. In Wales conducted very largely in the Welsh language. Came to have an important social and, to some extent, recreational function.
Test and Cor-poration Acts	Acts of 1661, 1673 and 1678 which prevented non-Anglicans from holding public office or being on municipal corporations. The Acts were repealed in 1828.
Tithe	That part of a landlord's or tenant's income paid to the established Church for its upkeep.
Tithe Com-mutation Act	Payment of tithes in kind (animals, crops, etc) was commuted to payment in money in 1836 by this Act.
Tithe War	The combination of land hunger, financial hardship and having to pay tithes to an alien church united Nonconformists, especially in north Wales, into direct opposition to Anglican landlords and to the established Church. Opposition included non-payment of tithes which led to confrontation.
Toll-Gates	These gates were erected on turnpike roads in the late eighteenth and early nineteenth centuries. Trusts were set up to build improved roads and were financed by tolls charged on animals and goods at the toll-gates.
Tory Party	Political party. In the nineteenth century generally associated with the establishment, whether the church or state, and conservative policies, though on

occasions had radical wings and sometimes implemented radical policies. Eventually became the Conservative Party. Opposed by the Liberal Party as a radical alternative.

Truck Shops   See *Company Shops.*

Turnpike Tolls   See *Toll-Gates.*

Union House   Normally refers to workhouses set up by groups or unions of parishes under the terms of the *Poor Law Amendment Act* of 1834. See *Poor Law.*

Unionism   Trade unionism.

Unitarians   Nonconformist religious denomination. Members believed in God but not in the divinity of Christ.

Vestry Room   Originally related to the room where the parish vestry, the equivalent of a local council, met. Developed into meaning an ante-room in a church or chapel where deacons' meetings and chapel functions were held.

Wakes Weeks   Traditional factory holidays in Lancashire and Yorshire when all factories and businesses closed down at the same time. The timing varied from town to town.

Welsh Calvinistic   See *Methodism.*
Methodists

Wesleyan   See *Methodism.*
Methodists

Wesleyans   See *Methodism.*

Western   Chartist newspaper published in Bath, 1839-40.
Vindicator

Wilkins, Charles   Merthyr ironmaster and historian. Wrote *History of Merthyr Tydfil* 1867, a source for the early history of the iron industry there. Also wrote *History of the Coal Trade of Wales* and *History of the Iron, Steel, Tinplate and other Trades of Wales.*

Whig	Political grouping in opposition to the Tories in the nineteenth century. Associated with radical policies. Developed eventually into the Liberal Party in the second half of the nineteenth century.
Working Men's Association	Established in 1836 by William Lovett and Henry Hetherington. Initiated the Charter from which *Chartism* eventually took its name. Hetherington was a close friend of Hugh Williams of Carmarthen (the solicitor who defended participants in the Rebecca Riots, and a Chartist) and in 1837 Williams became Secretary of the W.M.A. branch in Carmarthen. In 1838/9 about 50 branches of the W.M.A. were started in the south Wales coalfield. The movement fought to secure rights for the industrial working class.

Index

Index

Index

Index